For cops, the face of a missing child sums up all the terrible truths they learn on the job: innocent children, just like their own, disappear every day. Despite all the prayers and all the promises, some of those little boys and girls are found dead. Even worse, many more are never found at all.

This time, though, it was going to be different. It was going to be a gift—a joyous, wondrous gift. As the detectives peered down into the concrete tunnel, hoping against hope that little Katie Beers was still alive, each made a private vow: that no one, ever, would hurt Katie Beers again.

And then they heard a child's voice. They couldn't quite make out what she was saying, but they knew: It was Katie Beers.

She had beaten the odds. . . .

St. Martin's Paperbacks Titles by Joe Treen and Maria Eftimiades

"MY NAME IS KATHERINE"

St. Martin's Paperbacks Titles by Maria Eftimiades

LETHAL LOLITA

"My Name is KATHERINE"

THE TRUE STORY OF KATIE BEERS, THE LITTLE GIRL WHO SURVIVED AN UNDERGROUND DUNGEON OF HORROR

JOE TREEN and
MARIA EFTIMIADES

ST. MARTIN'S PAPERBACKS

"MY NAME IS KATHERINE"

Cover photograph by Ken Spencer/*New York Newsday*.

ISBN: 0-312-95188-4

Printed in the United States of America

St. Martin's Paperbacks edition/May 1993

10 9 8 7 6 5 4 3 2 1

Acknowledgments

Our thanks to *People* managing editor Landon Y. Jones for his enthusiastic support of this project. We also owe a debt of gratitude to *People* senior editors Howard Chua-Eoan and Jack Friedman and to chief of reporters Nancy P. Williamson for their patience and understanding. We are grateful for the assistance we received from Tom Apple, Paul Schreiber, Brad O'Hearn, the Suffolk County Police Department, and the East Hampton Township Police. We owe a debt of gratitude to our editor, Charles Spicer, his assistant, Liz Weinstock, St. Martin's managing editor John Rounds, copy-editor Ed Sedarbaum, and Elizabeth McNamara. We gratefully acknowledge the contributions of our indomitable agent, Jane Dystel. And we would especially like to thank Argiry Eftimiades and Jill Smolowe for all that they have done.

Chapter One

THE LITTLE GIRL flicked the channel selector on the television remote control with her thumb. Paula Zahn's face appeared on the screen. She hit the button again and got a commercial. Then Bryant Gumbel, then local news. She kept pushing the selector button, working her way through the channels, trying to deal with an unfamiliar mix of emotions: tedium and terror.

She was afraid of what Big John would do to her when he next came to see her. But she was even more afraid that he wouldn't come at all. That he would leave her here forever, all alone with no food or water, leave her here in this strange room to slowly starve to death.

The girl punched the channel selector again. *Ninja Turtles.* A Spanish-language station.

Sesame Street. Regular Thursday morning fare. Nothing special. She wished *Mister Ed* were on. It was her favorite show.

She thought about turning off the set. But it was her only company as well as her major source of light. There was also a tiny television monitor on the other side of the room, one that was connected to a hidden camera that showed what was going on outside. Otherwise the room was dark and damp. There were no windows and only one opening, a child-sized hatch, barely two feet square.

She studied the closed-circuit monitor for a moment. Nothing was happening outdoors. She could see the rear of the main house and the wooden gate that blocked the drive. No one was there. Not even Big John. All she could tell was that the sun had come up. She had survived another day.

The room was small, only six feet by seven feet, less space than the utility room in most suburban homes. But she didn't have even that much freedom. She was chained to the inside of a raised plywood box that Big John had built along one wall—a tomb-within-a-tomb, two feet high and three feet wide. She couldn't sit up. She couldn't move around. She couldn't do anything except flick channels with a remote control and wait for Big John to come.

She was thankful he had installed a TV set at the other end of the seven-foot-long box and hooked it up to cable. It gave her something to do. Ever since he had dragged her down here kicking and screaming three days ago, she had been following her own story on the news. Her picture was on every broadcast, either her fourth-grade school photo, the smiling one with her dark blond hair cut short, or the one from just a few days ago of her in a big floppy blossom hat about to blow out the candles on a birthday cake. She had seen her mother and her godmother, surrounded by cameras, pleading for her return. And she had watched Big John crying on the air because she was missing.

The girl pushed the channel selector a few more times. Home shopping. A workout class. Yesterday had been her tenth birthday. Today was New Year's Eve. Tomorrow might never come.

She could keep track of time from the TV and from her wristwatch. Big John had let her keep that. Sometimes she closed her eyes and pretended she was playing a *Home Alone* game. Other times, she thought about Dorothy in *The Wizard of Oz*. In the dark, she clicked her heels a few times.

The girl had no idea what Big John was planning to do with her, but it couldn't be good. From the beginning she had noticed those red stains on her mattress. Were they blood? Had some other child been here before her? Where was that child now?

Big John had always been nice to her before this, always nice to her brother, too. But now the little girl felt terror every time she heard him coming. First the one-way baby monitor in the room would crackle, "I'm coming down." Then it would be silent again while he opened the hatchway and dropped down a seven-foot shaft. Suddenly she would hear the whine of the battery-powered tool that he used to open the final doorway at the end of a short tunnel. It was so tight he had to squeeze through on his back.

He had brought her a salami sandwich or slices of pizza each time he came. The wrappings littered the floor, along with empty soda cans. If Big John brought nothing, she would really be afraid. And if he didn't come at all, she would die.

The girl glanced over at the closed-circuit monitor mounted on a shelf in the corner. Her heart began to race. Police cars had pulled up in front of the house. She couldn't hear their sirens but she could see the bubble lights on top, the insignias on the doors of the white cars. Dozens of policemen—uniformed and plainclothes—were everywhere, surrounding the main house, opening the wooden gate. She held her breath. Some of them were heading toward the barnlike garage that Big John had converted into living quarters. The dungeon was underneath that garage; the cement slab covering the vertical shaft was beneath a stereo cabinet in a tiny office off his kitchen.

The police were coming for her. Soon she would be free. For the first time in three days, the little girl smiled.

She pressed the remote and muted the volume on the television. She listened for the one-way baby monitor. Surely someone would be talking to her any second now. Surely someone would slither down the vertical shaft and through the tunnel and into the dungeon. She listened harder. There was only silence.

Her eyes never moved from the closed-circuit monitor. She could see the police going in and out of the main house. She could see them walking toward the garage, looking under the cover of the swimming pool, combing through leaves in the yard.

The girl began to scream. "Help! Please! I'm in here! I'm here!" She banged on the ceiling of her plywood coffin. She kicked the sides covered with corrugated foam rubber that made her feel as if she were living in an egg crate. She beat the ceiling with her reedlike arms. She yelled with all her might. "Let me out! I'm here! *I'm here!*"

She stopped. The silence terrified her. For the next four hours she watched the closed-circuit monitor in frustration and disbelief. They were looking for her—she knew it. All those policemen, their faces so somber. Now and then she could see Big John, nervously walking around. She could see him talking to the police, shaking his head, his hands jammed in his pockets.

Gradually the girl began to realize her greatest fear: the entrance to the dungeon was too well hidden. After all, she had been to Big John's house many times and, until three days ago, had had no idea it was there.

She tried yelling again, but her throat was aching. She never turned away from the closed-circuit television monitor. It was as if she thought that at any moment one of those policemen would look right at her and say, "There she is. She's alive!"

It never happened. An eternity passed, and the policemen left. She watched them walk to their cars. She saw them drive away.

The girl buried her head in the pillow and lay motionless. With the tiny bit of energy left in her body, she began to cry.

Chapter Two

THE BLACK 1989 Nissan pickup truck pulled up in front of a one-story ranch in Bay Shore, Long Island, and parked on the shoulder. The driver, a bald man with short brown hair on the sides, turned off the engine, picked up a gaily wrapped package from the front seat, and got out. It was sometime after 1:00 P.M., a gray drizzly day in late December.

The man calmly carried the present up the driveway to the mustard yellow house. At this time of year—three days after Christmas—there was nothing unusual about someone delivering a gift. But this one was different. Not only was it a *birthday* present, it was the beginning of a subtle mating dance, one that had to be kept secret because it was both illegal and disgusting. For John Esposito, forty-three, had come a-courting. And the object of his affections was a little girl, a child just two days shy of her tenth birthday.

There was no doorbell, so he knocked, sparking a torrent of dog barking inside. On the wooden door were the remains of a birthday party from the evening before: Mylar balloons and a sign that read, THE PARTY'S HERE! Above him was a tiny horseshoe that had been nailed into the white trim and painted over so many times it seemed to blend into the wood. The yellow shingles on the front of the house were cracked and faded, worn down from years of sea breezes off the Great South Bay just a mile to the south. The place seemed slightly rundown and seedy, as if the owners didn't live there and didn't really care.

Almost at once, a slight girl in a floppy blossom hat opened the screenless front door. She had short dark blond hair and a winning smile. She wore a dungaree skirt and a white blouse decorated with black Scottie dogs.

Behind her, two Pomeranians yapped noisily at the visitor, but like most dogs they were cowards and prudently kept their distance. John Esposito greeted the little girl warmly and stepped inside. He started to hand her the package but held it instead. Katie Beers was only four feet tall and weighed but fifty pounds. The present was almost as big as she was.

Inside the kitchen to the left, a heavyset woman in a wheelchair bellowed at the dogs to be quiet. She was an enormous woman with a flat coarse face and shoulder-length hair. Her name was Linda Inghilleri. She was thirty-eight but seemed older, as if every day of her hard life had left a mark on her appearance. She was tough-looking, like a bruiser who was cruising for a fight. Under her left eye was a blemish of some kind, which made her look as if she had just emerged from a fistfight. A plaid blanket covered her body from the lap down, but it did not hide the reason she was in a wheelchair. There was nothing where her left leg should have been.

Esposito followed Katie into the kitchen, where almost all business in the Inghilleri household transpired. He set the present down on the round wooden kitchen table and Linda smiled. Her own birthday was December 12; she knew that December babies were usually shortchanged when it came to birthdays. Children who came into the world at any other time of the year often got parties and presents. But kids born around Christmas got lost in the shuffle. They were an afterthought, a footnote, another holiday obligation. But John Esposito hadn't forgotten Katie Beers. Perhaps that is why Linda allowed him to visit her godchild that day. Despite her conflicting statements, Linda knew his reputation.

Katie Beers's tenth birthday would not be until December 30, two days away, but Linda had already made a fuss. Since Katie's visit with her this time was short—just a four-day stay between Christmas and New Year's—she had thrown the child a birthday party the evening before and invited all the kids from the neighborhood.

There had been a moment of tension, however. When Linda brought out the cake, it said, HAPPY BIRTHDAY, KATIE.

The little girl was upset. She'd made it clear to everyone in recent weeks that she preferred her *real* name. "My name is Katherine," she told her godmother. *"Katherine."*

But the strain passed quickly and someone began taking pictures. As always, Katie had worn her floppy blossom hat, the one she had kept on her head all the time since her mother, Marilyn, had shorn her of her waist-length locks two months before. Naturally, she was wearing it now.

John Esposito told Katie the present he had brought was for her. And Katie eagerly ripped off the wrapping. Inside was a huge brown box with the words "Barbie Dream House Furnished 1667–9993" printed on the side. Katie beamed. She loved Barbie dolls; this was just what she was hoping for. Esposito smiled too; he liked giving kids presents.

There was only one problem: it had to be assembled.

Esposito, a building contractor, would have no problem putting it together. In real life he built real houses; a dollhouse should be easy enough. But there wasn't much time. It was already pushing one-thirty in the afternoon and Esposito had also promised to take Katie to Toys "Я" Us to get her yet another birthday present. After that they were going to a big indoor amusement park called Spaceplex Family Fun Center. They would have to put the dollhouse together another time. Maybe when they got back.

If Katie was disappointed she didn't show it. She had known John Esposito as long as she could remember. His sister-in-law Joan—widow of his younger brother Patrick—knew Katie's mother, Marilyn. He was practically family.

Actually, he was better than family. He was like an uncle, but she never called him Uncle John. Like everyone else, she called him John in person. And like everyone else, she referred to him as Big John—though at five foot seven he wasn't particularly tall or heavy. Everyone called him Big John to distinguish him from John Beers, Katie's sixteen-year-old half brother. Katie's brother, of course, was known as Little John.

Big John had been taking Little John on outings practically every Sunday for the past nine years. In fact, that's where Esposito had been the night before, when Katie had suddenly become worried that he might not show up today, as he had promised. Katie knew that adults broke promises all the time. She was not yet ten but she could write a book on broken promises.

But Esposito had not forgotten. On that Sunday night he had taken Little John and two neighborhood kids—Anthony Frey, ten, and his sister Syndel, seven—to see *The Bodyguard*.

Back at his house, he had fixed a snack for the children and, around 9:00 P.M., gathered their coats and mittens and told them it was time to take them home. He had to work early the next day, he explained.

That wasn't true, and John Esposito knew it. He'd already planned to take the day off. It was easy for him. He and his twin brother, Ronald, owned their own business, J & R Home Improvements. Work had been slow lately anyway. Besides, it was the holiday week. The perfect time to relax at home.

Perhaps John Esposito had kept his plans to see Katie quiet so that the other children wouldn't be jealous. Maybe he was just tired, and thought a little white lie would make it easier to send the kids home early.

But perhaps there was another reason, one that he couldn't explain, not to anyone. For lately, John Esposito may have been suffering with a disturbing desire, one that he knew was wrong, terribly wrong.

Whatever his reason that night as he took the children home, John Esposito knew he had a date the following day: with Katie Beers.

He drove the Freys to their home in Central Islip. He couldn't stay, he told their mother, Kris Cosme. He had to take Little John to the Long Island Rail Road station in Bay Shore so the teen could catch the 10:10 back to his mother's house in Mastic, thirty-five miles east.

"I'm tired. I'm in no mood to drive all the way to Mastic," he explained to Kris. "I don't want this boy to miss his train."

Little John made the train with time to spare. When Esposito returned, he found a message from Katie on his answering machine: "John, give me a call tonight or tomorrow morning."

It was too late to call back that night. The next morning he phoned her at eleven.

"Can you pick me up?" she had asked anxiously. "Can we do something?"

John said they could. After all, he'd promised, hadn't he? Katie was delighted. Outings with Big John were always fun. Even just hanging around at Big John's house was wonderful. He kept an unlocked recreation room in the converted garage where he lived, just in case any kids from the neighborhood wanted to stop by, day or night. It was something of a children's paradise, with puzzles, a blow-up punching bag, a pool table, video games, a pink cassette player, a minibike, Nintendo, various board games, and bowls of candy. Few children could resist.

And Big John kept his promise, showing up that afternoon with Katie's present.

"You better get going," Linda told Katie and John.

"Right," said John, standing up.

Katie got her coat from the bedroom that Linda had fixed up especially for her. It was the perfect little girl's room, decorated in Disney, which Katie loved. The curtains and bedspread were from *One Hundred and One Dalmatians* and there were pictures on the wall from *Beauty and the Beast* and *Aladdin*.

When Katie came back, Linda gave her some letters to mail. And then Katie and John piled into Esposito's polished pickup truck and he started up the engine.

"Can I drive?" Katie asked.

"Sure," he said, and propped her up on his lap. Ocean Avenue was straight and wide, with nothing but tract houses on either side for a quarter mile or more. It was also empty; Ocean Avenue's spacious shoulders meant residents rarely parked their cars on the pavement. Letting an about-to-be-ten-year-old steer a slow-moving vehicle on this street was hardly dangerous. For Katie it was fun; for Esposito, perhaps, it was more like a date.

When they got to Bay Shore Boulevard, though, Esposito eased her onto the seat. This was a commercial road with fast-moving cars and trucks. He was a careful driver, with a clean record. He would have to have control of the pickup himself.

Ten minutes later he pulled into the parking lot of Toys "Я" Us on busy Sunrise Highway, a four-lane limited-access highway that runs along Long Island's South Shore. The toy store was not unlike thousands of others in the national franchise. It was in a large, rambling shopping center, just a mile or so from the summer ferry that sun-loving Manhattanites had been using for years to get to Fire Island.

Esposito found a parking place, but Katie didn't want to go inside right away. She had spotted several abandoned shopping carts in the lot. Each one was worth a quarter when returned to the store, and Katie was no fool. She quickly earned herself a dollar.

Once inside, it didn't take long for Katie to pick out her treasures. Her first stop was the video display between aisles 4A and 5A, next to children's clothes. There were nearly a hundred different videos to choose from—from Barney, the dinosaur, to *Beauty and the Beast*—but Katie knew exactly what she wanted: a $9.99 Barbie workout tape. She clutched it in her tiny hands as she hurried to the back of the store for the other item on her wish list: a Troll doll. Aisle 10C was full of them. Big. Little. In boxes. Stapled to cards. All of them had colorful shocks of hair, exaggerated noses, wide grins, shining eyes, and funny faces that made children (and adults) smile.

Katie carefully chose a $19.99 doll from a lower shelf. She weighed her decision carefully, spending a few minutes examining the enormous Barbie doll collection in a neighboring aisle before announcing that she had gotten what she came for.

But Esposito had a surprise. He walked Katie to the north end of the store, where computers and video games were sold. Aisle 2C was jammed with Nintendo software. Actually, the software itself wasn't there, only a picture of each of the games. Customers had to remove a ticket that looked a little like an automobile license plate from a blue envelope and present it to the cashier.

"So, which one do you want?" Esposito asked.

Katie was never one to hesitate. She promptly picked out the new *Home Alone 2* Nintendo game. The price tag read $49.99.

Katie Beers was not exactly a cheap date. She also picked out some items to give to "Aunt Lin"—Linda Inghilleri—and to her mother, Marilyn. In all, Esposito shelled out around a hundred dollars when they went through the cashier at the front of the store. But Esposito did not seem at all unhappy; he was always giving extravagant gifts to children. Besides, Katie was in heaven. She had once told a little girl her age that "men hurt you." But not Big John. He was kind and gentle. She took his hand as they walked out of the store to the pickup truck.

"Can we get a Slurpee?" she asked.

"Sure," Esposito said.

They got back into his truck and headed out of the lot. Instead of turning left toward Sunrise Highway, they went right on Brentwood Road. A few blocks later they pulled into a 7-Eleven tucked into a tiny lot in a residential zone.

Katie went to the rear of the store, next to the cold drink locker, picked up a paper cup, and stood on her tiptoes to make herself a Slurpee drink. She paid for it herself, giving the India-born clerk a five-dollar bill, then carefully placing the change into her small purse. Esposito stood beside her.

The original plan had been for them to continue north, to Nesconset and the Spaceplex amusement center, where Big John had taken Katie three times before. But Esposito had another idea.

"Why don't we take the video game back to my house and try it out first?" he suggested. "We've got plenty of time."

Katie nodded happily.

Esposito turned off Brentwood Road and wove through some residential streets toward his house, less than a mile away.

It was around 2:30 P.M., Monday, December 28. Sitting comfortably in the front seat of Big John's pickup truck that afternoon, little Katie Beers couldn't know that within an hour, her life would be irrevocably altered. For the next sixteen days she would not only fight to stay alive, she would struggle to retain her sanity. Nor could she know that the strange and twisted drama that was about to unfold would make her a household name across the nation.

Chapter Three

LINDA INGHILLERI was spending the afternoon of Monday, December 28, sitting at the round wooden table in her kitchen, doing what she did most afternoons: talking on the telephone.

She had made call after call, not taking a break until just after 5:00 P.M. Finally she hung up and rolled her wheelchair into another room to check on the progress of two sixteen-year-old boys from the neighborhood who were assembling Katie's new Barbie Dream House. Linda was paying them to put it together so it would be ready and waiting when her goddaughter got back at 6:00 P.M. She had no doubt that John Esposito would bring Katie back at that time. Big John was always punctual.

When she heard the phone start to ring, she knew she could never answer it in time. She was too far away. Even though her house was small, it wasn't easy to get from one end to the other in a wheelchair. Her friends knew to hold on even after the answering machine picked up.

As she wheeled herself back toward the kitchen table, she strained to hear who was calling. Maybe it was her mother or one of her sisters. Maybe it was Sal, her estranged husband. Maybe it was Katie and John. Maybe they were phoning to see if Katie could stay out later.

Linda was not prepared for what she heard next. Coming over her answering machine's speaker was the voice of a little girl, sobbing and screaming. The message was short and hard to understand but one thing was clear: whoever was calling needed help. Then the girl's voice cut off abruptly and the call terminated.

"Katie! Katie!" Linda shouted. There could be no question. That was Katie's voice. Something was terribly wrong.

Linda rushed to the answering machine on her kitchen table. The two teenagers heard her cries and hurried to her side.

She grabbed the white telephone next to the machine. "Hello! Hello!" she shouted. But it was too late. All Linda could hear was a dial tone. She slammed down the phone, rewound the machine, and played the message again.

On second hearing, the words were much clearer—and more alarming. As she listened, Linda felt a chill race through her body. She could hardly breathe.

"I've been kidnapped by a man with a knife, and oh, my God, here he comes—"

Linda started to become hysterical. She rewound the machine again and replayed the message, listening for something that might alleviate her fears, anything that might convince her someone was playing a cruel joke. She repeated the process several times, screaming and sobbing each time she heard little Katie's cry for help.

This was no joke. This was for real. Katie was in trouble.

Finally, Linda composed herself enough to pick up the telephone and make a call.

The Spaceplex Family Fun Center in Nesconset, Long Island, looks like an amusement park inside an airplane hanger. There are bumper cars, a Tilt-a-Whirl, a minijet, and miniature golf—all under a ceiling thirty-two and a half feet high. One area resembles a county fair, with a shooting gallery and a game where players try to knock over stacked bowling pins with a baseball. Everywhere else, it seems, are elaborate video games and pinball machines.

But the rides and games are only part of the attraction. The place feels like a discotheque. To get inside, patrons must pass through a long hallway lit only with blinding strobe lights. Hard rock music blares from superloud speakers. And, inside the 3.2-acre structure, it is perpetual evening, with red, black, and gray walls, gray carpets, and subdued lighting. Children love it. So do adults.

During the week between Christmas and New Years, the Spaceplex Family Fun Center was packed. There was no school and many businesses had shut down for the holidays. So, even though it was a Monday afternoon, technically a working day, more than five hundred kids and their parents were crowded inside.

Theresa Brosnan, forty-four, Spaceplex weekend party manager, was sitting in her office when her phone rang.

"Good evening, Spaceplex, may I help you?"

On the other end of the line a hysterical woman started to scream. "Get security! Get the owner! Lock all the exits!" the woman yelled. "There's a man dragging a nine-year-old girl at knifepoint out of Spaceplex!"

Brosnan had never received a call like this before in her life, but she kept her wits about her.

"What's your name?" she asked. If this were

a crank call, she figured, the woman would never give her name.

"Linda Inghilleri," the caller said forthrightly. "Hurry!"

"Hold on," Theresa said, trying to be reassuring and calm, like an airline pilot in the middle of a storm.

She got up from her desk, still holding the phone, and peered down the strobe-lit hallway. Nothing was unusual, only customers coming and going. There certainly was no man dragging a little girl out of the building at knifepoint.

What kind of drugs is this one on? she asked herself. This has to be a joke.

At that moment Neil Golden, a security guard, happened by. Theresa motioned to him. "Take this call," she ordered.

As Neil spoke to the woman, he looked up at the ceiling and rolled his eyes. This can't be going on here, he was thinking.

"Get her phone number," Theresa told him. After he jotted it down, Theresa took the phone again. "Okay, we'll call you right back," she said.

With that, Theresa Brosnan instigated a search. She went into the main arena and sent one of her staff members to check the girls' bathroom. Then Theresa went out to the parking lot. She looked inside each of the twenty-five or so cars parked in the lot.

"Katie?" she called repeatedly. "Katie?"

She even went to the rear of the building, continuing to call out Katie's name.

In Bay Shore, meanwhile, Linda Inghilleri was not sitting by idly. She listened to the tape one more time, then dialed 911.

All 911 calls in Suffolk County are routed to a large room on the second floor of police headquarters in Yaphank, not far from the famed Brookhaven National Laboratory.

Yaphank, which is in roughly the geographic center of Suffolk County, houses an enormous complex of governmental buildings including the Board of Elections, the Public Works Department, the county infirmary, and police headquarters. Anyplace else this might be the county seat, but not in Suffolk. Because the county is long and narrow, with Texas-sized proportions—1,170 square miles—Suffolk has *three* governmental centers, one on either end and Yaphank in the middle.

Linda's call went to Chris Glynn, one of a dozen emergency complaint officers, or ECOs. Glynn was wearing headphones and sitting in front of a computer, but much of his job was not electronic at all. His first action was to stamp the time of Linda's call on a blank Central Complaint card, or CC. It was 5:14 P.M.

Returning to the conversation, he punched Linda's name and address into the computer, which automatically told him which police sector and precinct Linda lived in. After that he filled out—by hand—CC card No. 92-651-683, giving name, address, and type of crime. In this case it was a ten-thirty-one, a missing person.

With that, he stuck the card into the time clock again to record when he had finished the call. And then he put the card in one of several chutes next to him, one leading to the dispatcher for the Fourth Precinct, which covered the Spaceplex Family Fun Center.

The card slid along the chute into the next room, where it was stopped by one of the lowest-tech tools in the annals of modern police science: a piece of foam. The dispatcher punched in the time she received the card and checked her map. Part of her job was to know where each squad car in the precinct was and what it was handling. She immediately called car 403, the closest available.

"Four oh three. Four zero three," she said into the microphone in front of her.

The answer came back immediately. "Four oh three."

"I have a ten-thirty-one. Investigate a possible missing person. Juvenile. Katie Beers. At Spaceplex, 620 Route 25, Nesconset. Complainant is Linda Inghilleri"—she spelled out Linda's name.—"at 1083 Ocean Avenue, Bay Shore. Says she received a call saying the child has been kidnapped."

"Ten-four."

For all its arcane methods, the Suffolk emergency response system works well. Car 403 was on its way within minutes of Linda's call.

At that very moment, John Esposito was inside the Spaceplex Family Fun Center, looking worried. He rushed up to floor manager Mike Gottlieb in the billiards room, an area with sixteen gray felt pool tables.

"I'm looking for a little girl," Esposito said. "I can't find her."

"We'll page her," Mike said without hesitation. This was not the first child to wander away from an adult at Spaceplex; he knew exactly what to do.

"What's her name?"

"Katie Beers."

Mike picked up the telephone, punched in the letters ICM—for *intercom*—followed by the numbers 8 and 5. That put him on the Spaceplex loudspeaker system.

"Katie Beers. Please report to the billiard room. Katie Beers, please come to the billiard room."

Esposito and Gottlieb waited several minutes but Katie did not show up.

"I'll do it again," Mike said without being asked.

Again Katie did not appear, but this time Mike's call brought to the scene another manager, Theresa Abbazia, thirty-one, who had worked at Spaceplex since its opening two years before.

"What's happened?" she asked.

"I went to pinball, she went to Skee-Ball," Esposito said unhappily.

"I haven't seen her since."

"We'll find her," Abbazia said with a reassuring smile. "Don't worry."

A few minutes later Theresa Brosnan came back into the Spaceplex building after searching the parking lot. Neil Golden, the security guard, greeted her as she came through the door.

"We paged her," he said. "But she didn't respond."

Theresa went back to her office and reluctantly called Linda. She wasn't eager to deal with an overbearing and hysterical woman.

Much to Theresa's relief, Linda sounded calmer.

"Could you give me a better description of the child?" Theresa asked.

Linda quickly described Katie: four feet tall, fifty pounds, short blond hair, a floppy hat.

"Did you drop her off here alone?" Theresa asked. Parents routinely left their kids at Spaceplex for the afternoon. The drop-off trade was a major part of the amusement center's business.

"No, no," Linda corrected. "She's with a man friend of mine. John."

"How old is the man friend?" Theresa asked.

"Forty-three or forty-four."

Theresa implored the heavens with a fast look at the ceiling. *You've got to be kidding!* she thought to herself.

"Did he call you?" she asked.

"No."

"Then how do you know he even got here?"

"He said he was going there."

"What's his name again?"

"John Esposito."

"Okay. I'll call you back."

Theresa hung up and punched in ICM 85 on her office phone. "John Esposito, to the party office. John Esposito, to the party office," she said into the receiver.

But this time it was John Esposito who didn't answer the page. Theresa gave him a few minutes. When he didn't show up, she left her office and walked through the strobe-lit hallway to the main arena where there was another paging line, one that was usually clearer. She paged Esposito again. Still he did not show up.

But Neil Golden, who had just searched the entire game area a second time, did. The two walked back to Theresa's office. Waiting for them was a man in his early forties.

"Are you John Esposito?" Theresa asked.

Esposito looked alarmed. "How do you know my name?" he asked quickly, too quickly as far as Theresa was concerned.

"Linda called," she said. "Where is Katie?"

"Oh. She's gone," John said. "She disappeared."

"You better call Linda."

Esposito looked even more alarmed. "I don't know her number," he said.

If it was a stalling tactic, it didn't work.

"Here it is," Theresa said, handing Esposito a piece of paper.

He dialed the number on Theresa's office phone and spoke to Linda for several minutes.

It was a one-sided conversation, with Linda doing almost all the talking.

"I don't know," John said, when he could get

a word in. "She's gone, . . . No. . . . Yeah. . . . Yeah. . . . Uhh-huh. . . . Yeah."

While Esposito talked on the phone, Theresa Brosnan decided it was time to get more help. No lost-child incident at Spaceplex had ever gone on this long or been this complicated. Children were invariably reunited with their parents within minutes.

She went next door into the main office of Spaceplex. Inside, Kelly Clelland, twenty-eight, a manager since the amusement center opened in October 1990, was working at her desk.

"Did you hear what happened?" Theresa asked.

"What?"

"A girl is missing."

Kelly and Theresa walked back to the party office together as John was hanging up the phone. He was standing.

Clelland, on gut instinct alone, mistrusted Esposito from the start. "What happened?" she asked him.

"This little girl I brought here is missing. Her name is Katie Beers. I've been paging her. She hasn't responded."

"Can you give us a description?" she asked.

"Well . . ." Esposito seemed uncomfortable. "She had a skirt on, and, uh, a white shirt."

"We really need to get some more detail," Kelly said curtly.

"Her aunt would have a better description of her," Esposito suggested.

"Tell me again what happened."

"I was at pinball, she was—" Suddenly he was interrupted by a page on the loudspeaker. "John Esposito, you have a phone call."

It was Linda, calling back. John took the phone, but he looked as if he were about to cry. He handed the receiver to Kelly without a word.

"We need a better description," Kelly told Linda.

Kelly began to write down the things Linda told her. Denim skirt, white shirt with Scottie dogs on the sleeves, black boots, short dark blond hair, floppy hat.

"The cops are on their way here," Linda told Kelly. "Oh, here they are now."

A minute later a cop got on the phone. "We're sending officers over there from the Fourth Precinct," he said. "They'll be there right away."

The Spaceplex employees glanced at each other, puzzled by the escalating events. They looked at John Esposito. He turned his head away, and seemed to be crying.

Only two people—John Esposito and Katie Beers—knew what had happened in his Bay

Shore home that afternoon. Now, as he waited for the police to arrive, John Esposito was grasping for the first time that there would be no turning back. The odyssey of little Katie Beers had just exploded into the public arena.

Chapter Four

IT TOOK NO TIME at all for the cops to arrive at Spaceplex. In New York City, just fifty miles to the west, police might not react as quickly over a lost child. But this was suburbia, where children were the lifeblood of the community. Car 403 from Suffolk County's Fourth Precinct in nearby Hauppauge, Long Island, turned off Middle Country Road and was racing down the amusement center's long driveway within minutes.

Peter Germond and his partner had just started their tour, the four-to-twelve shift, when they got the call. As soon as they arrived at the Spaceplex center, Germond talked to Linda Inghilleri by phone while his partner took a quick tour of Spaceplex, which was jammed with patrons having a good time.

By now it was 5:45 P.M. and dark outside. Several of the eight Spaceplex managers on duty went outside to scour the parking lot. Meanwhile, more cops arrived. Some were from the juvenile division, others from missing persons. They gathered in the small office where employees booked birthday parties. Esposito sat on a side bench. Kelly Clelland and Theresa Brosnan both leaned against the desk.

"Do you want something to drink?" Kelly asked Esposito.

"Yeah, coffee," he said offhandedly. "Black, two sugars."

He seemed both helpless and hopeless, always looking as if he were on the verge of tears. Rock music from inside the gigantic hall added to the pathos; the proximity of hundreds of people having fun only seemed to make things worse.

But, even so, those inside the party office were having a hard time believing Esposito.

"He looked like he was pretending to be upset," Kelly recalled later. "Every time he went to cry, he covered his eyes or turned away. He seemed a little bit strange. Not your average Joe. It's hard to make a judgment whether he was upset or faking."

After a while Germond and his partner took Esposito out to a patrol car and sat with him, asking questions. Eventually the officers walked Esposito over to his Nissan pickup truck. They noticed how neat and clean it was, how it was bright and shiny even in winter.

Inside the cab, in the area behind the front seat, were Katie's coat—and hat.

Esposito, the cops said later, looked genuinely surprised.

At 6:30 P.M., Gary Tuzzalo raced into the Spaceplex parking lot. He and six partners had opened the amusement center just over two years ago, but he generally ran the place. Tuzzalo had left Spaceplex that night just minutes before Esposito asked Mike Gottlieb to page Katie.

Kelly Clelland had called his beeper and punched in the office phone number at Spaceplex followed by 911. Tuzzalo had just arrived at his mother's house and was sitting down for dinner. She was serving pasta. He looked down at his beeper, surprised.

Tuzzalo phoned Spaceplex immediately. The 911 made him nervous.

"What's up?" he asked.

Kelly quickly filled him in. Tuzzalo listened in silence.

"What's the matter?" his mother asked as he set the phone back on its cradle.

"They said a little girl is missing," he said, shaking his head in amazement. "There's no way, Mom. She's either there or something's up. You can't get a kid out of there. There's too much security, in and out."

"You better get going, Gary," his mother said evenly.

He knew she was right.

"Okay, Mom, I'm outta here."

Now that he had returned to Spaceplex, Gary Tuzzalo only had one thing on his mind. He went straight to the cops. It was impossible, he insisted, to drag a child out of the amusement center at the point of a knife. "Something's fishy," he said. "There's no way that could happen here."

A detective agreed. Tuzzalo was *probably* right. But what if he wasn't? What if, somehow, someone had kidnapped Katie Beers? What if her little body was lying in the fields or in the woods surrounding the building? What if she was injured and not dead? What if she had run away and gotten lost?

There were too many possibilities and every one of them had to be checked out. A child's life was at stake. A nine-year old girl.

Tuzzalo knew the detective was right. He promptly asked the private security company that patrolled Spaceplex to send over additional manpower. Cadets from the police academy in North Babylon also arrived. Kelly Clelland photocopied a description of Katie and handed it out, and the search crews fanned out into the dark, foggy night. They were soon joined by a K-9 team—a dog and a handler—and by two police helicopters, which would play their searchlights across the woods surrounding the amusement center.

Meanwhile, a group of Spaceplex employees systematically went through the amusement center—which was still crowded with customers happily unaware of what was going on. They found nothing. They couldn't even find anyone who had *seen* her.

At 7:30 P.M. a police officer who had been at Linda Inghilleri's house in Bay Shore arrived. He brought with him a copy of Katie's terrifying kidnapping message recorded on Linda's answering machine.

"We want you to hear this tape," the cop said. "We want to see if you recognize any sounds."

Three or four Spaceplex employees and three or four cops gathered in the main office and listened carefully. Esposito was not present. He was next door in the Spaceplex party office, being questioned by detectives.

"It doesn't sound like Spaceplex," Gary Tuzzalo said immediately. "I'm here all the time and I know the sounds of this building."

Kelly Clelland agreed. "That's not our

sound," she told the officers. "You work here two years, you know the background noises. That wasn't made here. It sounds like it was made from the road."

Kelly didn't say what she was really thinking. "The tape didn't sound real," she said later. "I didn't want to say anything. It would have sounded kind of cruel. But everyone knew the call wasn't made here."

"Listen to it again," the police suggested. And they did. The Spaceplex employees heard Katie's hysterical words six more times. They were never swayed: that tape could not have been made at Spaceplex.

"It doesn't make sense," Gary Tuzzalo kept saying. "How could this be? A man with a knife is chasing her and she runs for a phone? Why is she running for a phone? Why isn't she running for help? This doesn't make sense at all."

The cops nodded slowly. They were thinking exactly the same thing.

At about 8:00 P.M. that Monday evening, Kris Cosme returned to her Central Islip home from her job driving a bus along the South Shore of Suffolk County. Her wheelchair-bound husband, Juan, had been listening to the family's Radio Shack police scanner. Radio traffic was unusually heavy that night, he told his wife. A child was missing. A girl from Bay Shore named Katie Beers.

"My God," Kris gasped. "That's my friend Marilyn's daughter."

"Which one is Marilyn?" asked Juan, confused. He and Kris had been married only a few months. His wife's many friends were still something of a blur to him.

"Little John's mother."

"My God." Juan knew Little John. Even though the teen was six years older than Kris's son Anthony, the two boys were still good friends. They often did things together with their mutual "big brother," John Esposito.

The couple talked about Katie late into the night. "I bet she ran away," Kris told her husband. After all, she explained, little Katie had every reason to want to flee her troubled life.

In nearby Bay Shore, at the home of Linda Inghilleri, Suffolk police officers were also considering the possibility that Katie Beers had run away. Statistically it was unlikely. Studies show that children under the age of thirteen rarely disappear on their own.

But there had been a minor disagreement the night before between Katie and her godmother. Katie had been upset that her birthday cake read HAPPY BIRTHDAY, KATIE! rather than HAPPY BIRTHDAY, KATHERINE!

Was that enough to inspire a child to run away? police officers asked.

Who knew these days? one of them answered.

Marilyn Beers didn't find out that her daughter was missing until around 8:30 that evening. She had just gotten home when her landlord knocked on the door of her one-bedroom apartment in Mastic Beach, a down-on-its-luck village on Suffolk County's South Shore. She lived in what had once been a two-car garage. Years ago, the owner of the rambling ranch house on the corner of Mill Drive and Pineway Avenue had converted it into an apartment to pick up some extra cash. He didn't ordinarily take calls for Marilyn. But this was an emergency. Katie had disappeared. Marilyn was supposed to call Linda Inghilleri at once.

She trotted down the wooden stoop of her tiny apartment and up the walkway to her landlord's kitchen. Like Linda Inghilleri, Marilyn Beers, forty-four, was an enormous woman. She had fat arms, a protruding stomach, and a round face with a double chin. Her eyes were narrow and suspicious behind thin-rimmed aviator glasses. And she kept her waist-length hair pulled back severely from her face in a tight ponytail. She looked like a pleasant woman who had nothing to be pleasant about. She was cold, distant. And she never seemed to smile.

When Marilyn first moved into the garage in October 1991, it had been perfect for her and her teenaged son, John. But three months later her mother, Helen Beers, and Katie came to live there too. Four people made a one-bedroom apartment crowded. Conditions were squalid, with mattresses piled on the floor, unwashed dishes stacked high in the sink, and trash strewn everywhere. Marilyn was no housekeeper.

She had no car, and worst of all as far as Marilyn was concerned, she had no phone. The New York Telephone Company wouldn't give her any service—not after someone in her household had run up bills in the thousands of dollars.

When Marilyn reached Linda on the phone, the news was both alarming and shocking. Her daughter was missing; she might have been kidnapped. Added to that terrible pain was hurt. Marilyn learned that Katie had been out with John Esposito that day. A year earlier she had forbidden her two children to see Esposito, and she had made sure that Linda knew it. Although Marilyn was aware that Little John had paid no attention to her ban and frequently visited Esposito, she didn't know that Katie was seeing him as well.

Despite their years of friendship, Marilyn no longer approved of Big John. She didn't want her children going near him. Not since Little John had told her what John Esposito had been doing to him for years.

But that night she held her tongue. She immediately called her friend Teddy Rodriguez, Little John's father, and he picked her up in his Dodge. They sped down Sunrise Highway to Bay Shore and waited by the phone with Linda and the police.

Little John stayed home in Mastic. All this sounded crazy to him. Katie kidnapped? Yet somehow he wasn't surprised that John Esposito was involved. "I had this strange gut feeling it was Esposito," he said later. "I knew it from day one."

Many cops had that feeling too. What they didn't have was proof. They weren't even sure exactly what John Esposito might or might not have done. Some theorized that Esposito might have helped Katie run away. Others speculated that he had killed her. Most of the detectives assigned to the case, however, believed the same scenario: Esposito had tried to molest

Katie and things had gone badly. "She panics, he panics," one cop said. "If this comes out, he knows he's in big trouble. So she ends up dead."

All the police knew for sure was that a little girl was missing, that Esposito's story didn't seem to tally, and that he acted strangely. They questioned him late into the evening at Spaceplex.

His version of the last two days' events never varied. He described how Katie had called him the night before, how he had picked her up at Linda Inghilleri's house, how they had gone shopping at Toys "Я" Us and stopped for a Slurpee at the 7-Eleven.

Esposito readily admitted that he had taken Katie to his house to play the *Home Alone 2* video game but said that it turned out not to be that much fun. After only fifteen minutes, he insisted, they decided to go to the Spaceplex.

They had arrived around 4:30 P.M., he said. As they walked through the strobe-lit hallway, he gave Katie a five-dollar bill. The two were going to go their separate ways, their usual practice when they went to Spaceplex.

Katie headed off to buy tokens for the various games, John said, and he held on to her coat and hat. "That's the last time I seen her, when she was walking to the machine," he said. "I went to the pinball machine. I played about three video games and I would just look over and see where she was. I didn't see her. I didn't think too much about it."

At least not at first. After thirty minutes, Esposito said, he started to get worried. "I was getting scared," he told detectives. "I couldn't find her. It's a big place. I'm going crazy looking all over. Then I went to security. 'Could you page Katie Beers?' They did it about three times."

John Esposito was getting tired. He'd repeated this same story countless times. He was relieved when the cops finally told him to go home.

When he did, a team of detectives was right behind him.

Chapter Five

WHEN DAWN filtered through the thick fog the next morning, Katie Beers had still not been found. At 7:00 A.M., visibility at Long Island MacArthur Airport—not far from the Spaceplex Family Fun Center—was a quarter of a mile. By noon, Long Island was still fogged in. This was not going to be an easy day to find anyone.

The police waited to see if the fog would lift. But the press corps didn't. A pack of reporters, photographers, and cameramen had arrived in full force at Spaceplex by 9:00 A.M.

If a nine-year-old girl had disappeared 50 miles due *west* of New York—almost to Pennsylvania—the city's giant media machine might not have noticed. But this was Long Island. As much as the 2.7 million residents in the 516 area code chafed at being in the shadow of the Big Apple, there was no getting around the fact that Long Island was considered a New York City suburb—all the way out to Montauk Point, 120 miles from Manhattan.

Besides, this was also Amy Fisher country. The Long Island teenager had shot her alleged lover's wife, Mary Jo Buttafuoco, in Massapequa, less than 25 miles from where Katie Beers had been growing up. Fisher had already been the subject of countless newspaper and television reports, a *People* magazine cover story, and a book called *Lethal Lolita.* A day earlier, December 28, the first of three "movies of the week" about the teen call girl was going to air on NBC. The Amy Fisher saga had seemingly gone beyond the saturation point and yet the interest level in her case kept getting higher, not lower. Now, the New York City press corps had a fresh mystery. Indeed, many of the same reporters who had camped out on Joey Buttafuoco's sidewalk were now greeting each other in the parking lot of the Spaceplex amusement center. It was Old Home Week in the fog.

At 6:00 A.M. the phone on Kris Cosme's bedside table started to ring. She was still asleep when she answered it but woke up the minute she heard who was calling. It was a Suffolk County detective.

"We're investigating the disappearance of Katie Beers, and we understand your son has been associated with John Esposito," he said.

Kris didn't particularly like the tone of his question; she was a fan of John Esposito. She still is. But she expressed her displeasure indirectly. "Yeah?" she said. "Couldn't you have at least waited until seven-thirty, when I was awake?"

The detective managed to be both unapologetic and polite at the same time. "Do you want me to call you back?" he asked.

"No, you got me up," Kris said. "Just lemme just get a cup of coffee."

She slipped out of bed, grabbed her robe, and padded into the kitchen at the front of her house. It turned out to be a long conversation. She told the detective about her children's relationship with John Esposito, how her two older children—Anthony Frey, ten, and Syndel Frey, seven—spent time with him regularly. He was informally their "big brother"; he took them places, did things with them. He had just taken them to see *The Bodyguard* two nights before. He had been doing things like that regularly ever since she and her first husband, Martin Frey, split up in 1990. And she was very grateful.

When she hung up, around 9:00 A.M., she

immediately made another call—to John Esposito.

"Are you all right?" she asked.

"I'm okay," he responded. "I can't talk."

John Esposito was right. He couldn't talk. He was with the cops—or rather the cops were with him. They had been questioning him nonstop since squad car 403 arrived at the Spaceplex Family Fun Center the previous evening. The session in the amusement center had gone on until late. Now they were in his house. They had been there all night.

Like the Beers family, Esposito lived in a converted garage. But his was nothing like the cramped quarters Katie shared with her mother, brother, and grandmother in Mastic Beach. His originally had been a small barnlike shed behind his family's home in Bay Shore, the house he had grown up in. An excellent carpenter, he had gradually transformed the place into a bungalow, adding rooms, a second story, and then, about a year ago, a yellow carport on the back.

The house had five rooms, including a bedroom, a living room, and a kitchen with a little office right off it. But the room that attracted the most notice from the three detectives who were with him was the second-floor rec room.

It was crammed with everything from Nintendo games to bowls of candy. When Esposito explained that he kept the rec room open at all times so that neighborhood kids could come over and play, the detectives all glanced at each other but said nothing.

With Esposito's permission the detectives looked through the house and instantly found something important—Katie's handbag—on a shelf. When they showed it to Esposito he seemed confused, just as he had when police discovered Katie's hat and coat in his pickup truck.

But for the three detectives, the pocketbook spoke volumes. Even nine-year-old girls did not leave their handbags behind. Either Katie had never left Esposito's house that afternoon—or she hadn't left the place alive. Esposito obviously had done something with her. Maybe he had killed her, or maybe he had hidden her somewhere. Perhaps he was trying to shield her from her warring family members. Maybe he actually did have her best interests in mind. One thing, however, was certain: John Esposito was the police's prime suspect. No doubt about that.

Whenever a police investigation gets to this point, the logical next step is to start leaning. Make the suspect crack. Detectives rely on confessions. They have to. Developing a case on physical evidence alone is both difficult and chancy. It is unlikely to lead to a conviction. Or, in this case, to a missing girl.

But Esposito wouldn't crack. No matter how hard the detectives pushed him, he stuck to his story. He went over it many times, deviating only slightly.

He did volunteer one bit of information that made the detectives all the more certain they had the right man. He told them that he had a criminal record. In 1977, he explained, he had been arrested for leading a seven-year-old boy out of the Sunrise Mall shopping center in Massapequa. He had pleaded guilty to unlawful imprisonment, a misdemeanor, and had received probation. Nothing like that had ever happened since, he assured the officers.

But it only whetted their desire to conclude the case. The questions came faster and faster. The cops wanted Esposito to crack.

By late morning the police decided to go ahead with a ground search for Katie Beers, fog or no fog. Visibility wasn't improving; if anything it was getting worse. But if a child was out there in the woods and fields around Spaceplex, time was not something that could be squandered. Search parties were formed from a busload of cadets from the police academy in North Babylon, along with numerous volunteers, including Gary Tuzzalo and Kelly Clelland of Spaceplex. They were joined by two K-9 teams—each a German shepherd and a handler.

But by midafternoon everyone knew it was useless. The search parties had looked in every conceivable place where a nine-year-old girl might hide—or be hidden: abandoned buildings, public storage areas, buses at a local bus company, and Dumpsters, plenty of Dumpsters. "We checked every Dumpster from Stony Brook Road to Edgewood Avenue in Smithtown, a seven-mile stretch," said a weary Inspector Dominick Steo, Fourth Precinct commander and search coordinator. They had found nothing.

At 1:20 that afternoon John Esposito decided he had had enough. He told the detectives he wanted to call his lawyer, Sidney Siben of Siben & Siben in Bay Shore, the attorney who had represented him when he was arrested in 1977. Sidney Siben had been practicing law for fifty-seven of his eighty-one years. He had long passed the point where he took guff from anyone.

"The cops are here, at my house," Esposito told Siben over the phone.

"How many?" Siben asked.

"Three detectives."

"How long have they been there?"

"It's been eighteen hours."

"Eighteen hours!" Siben exclaimed, wondering why Esposito hadn't called him sooner. "Have you had any sleep?"

"No."

"Put one of them on."

Esposito handed the phone to one of the detectives.

"I'm Sidney Siben," Siben said. "I'm Mr. Esposito's attorney."

The detective introduced himself and Siben got straight to the point. "Do you have a warrant for my client's arrest?"

"No," the detective said.

"Do you have a search warrant?"

"No."

Siben didn't mince words. "Then get out," he commanded. And the detectives did.

At police headquarters in Yaphank, Deputy Inspector Kenneth Rau decided to activate for the first time a special kidnapping task force that had been created three years before.

Just before Thanksgiving in 1989, a young

mentally retarded boy had been snatched from his parents' home in Farmingville, a bedroom community in the central part of the Island that had once been potato-farming country. Suffolk police readily admit that detectives were fumbling around in the dark on that investigation; they had had little experience with kidnappings. Many mistakes were made.

As it happened, the retarded boy was recovered in good condition, but police officials weren't patting themselves on the back. They decided instead to have a group of detectives trained by the FBI and New York City police in techniques for handling kidnapping cases.

In all, thirty-nine detectives and investigators were chosen for the task force. After their schooling, they simply returned to their regular jobs throughout the department. But if a kidnapping case came up, they were to drop whatever they were doing and begin a special investigation.

Detective Lieutenant Dominick Varrone headed the task force. Ordinarily he was in charge of the detective unit in the First Precinct, which covered the Babylon Township, the westernmost on Suffolk's south shore. Short, stocky, with dark hair and mustache, Varrone looked every bit a detective as he directed his team and dealt with myriad press inquiries. He had a special interest in this case. One of his own children was a ten-year-old girl. Her name was Katherine.

Other detectives on the task force had very specific responsibilities. Some were involved in electronic eavesdropping, others in canvassing neighborhoods. Still others were assigned the job of working with the phone company, setting up wiretaps and tracing equipment to track any ransom calls that might come in.

Another part of the program was the FBI, which offered technical assistance and expertise. It provided the first nugget of information. An FBI voice analysis confirmed that the phone call received by Linda Inghilleri had been made by Katie Beers. But the central question remained: Where was she?

At 5:30 A.M., Police Officer David Bloom of the Suffolk County Police Department's public information office put out a press release. He walked over to the Cannon fax machine in the lobby of police headquarters in Yaphank and put the one-page document into the machine.

With the push of a button, the fax went out simultaneously to seventy news organizations on Long Island and in New York City.

There was a glitch, however. The press release misspelled Katie's first name, giving her two "*ts*" instead of one. Almost every copy desk in the metropolitan area caught the error. But there were exceptions. The Long Island edition of *Newsday* ran the incorrect version of the little girl's name in a caption on the front page the next day. Even worse, the New York *Daily News* continued to misspell her name in headlines and stories for the next two weeks.

The press release, only 127 words long, was written in police-ese with a Long Island accent:

> The Suffolk County Police Department is asking the public for their assistance in locating Kattie Beers, a 9-year-old Mastic resident, missing under circumstances evincing an abduction.
>
> Kattie was last seen on Monday, December 28, at approximately 4:30 p.m. at the Spaceplex Family Center, Rt. 25, Nesconset.
>
> She is a white female, 4 feet tall, 50 pounds, light complexion, brown eyes, with short straight dirty blonde hair. She had a small hole in her right cheek from minor surgery. When last seen Kattie was wearing a dungaree skirt, white shirt with black Scottie dogs, and black boots.
>
> Anyone with information concerning

> the whereabouts of Kattie Beers can contact the Fourth Squad detectives at 854-8452, or the juvenile/missing persons section at 852-6195.

The release made a big story even bigger; an official press release sometimes does wonders to help a story along. Producers and editors have something tangible to look at while awaiting electronic copy and videotape to arrive.

That night on television the story was at the top of the local news. Katie's picture, taken in her fourth-grade class just a few weeks before she disappeared, was broadcast into millions of homes throughout the New York metropolitan area. It was a nice picture in front of a backdrop of trees and mountains. She was wearing a suitlike dress with a wide collar and four brass buttons. And she was looking slightly off to her left, smiling shyly. She looked like the perfect child.

There was also footage of search teams with dogs patrolling around Spaceplex. Marilyn Beers and Linda Inghilleri were on camera, tearfully begging for Katie's safe return. Even John Esposito spoke out. Rubbing his face with his hand, he said how much he loved Katie, how much he wanted her back. "Just find the girl," he said, his voice breaking. Each station displayed a special telephone number for people to call if they had seen the missing girl.

Watching it all was Katie Beers. In the cramped box that had become her home, she sat frustrated and worried. She knew where she was but she couldn't tell anyone. She hoped she wouldn't get into trouble for all the fuss that was going on. But there was one thing she knew for sure. Big John had been lying to her. He hadn't put her down here to protect her from her mother and Aunt Lin. That's what he had told her. But she now knew that was just an excuse. His real motives were still a mystery. Little Katie Beers could only wonder—and tremble at the uncertainty.

Chapter Six

JOHN ESPOSITO may have been the police's prime suspect, but that didn't mean that detectives could stop there. They had to cover every base—and what they were quickly discovering was that they had a lot of bases to cover. For a girl just turning ten years old, Katie Beers had been living an extraordinarily complicated and difficult life.

Statistically, Detective Dominick Varrone knew, the odds were good Katie was still alive. Most kidnapped children are abducted by family members—usually in a custody dispute—and the survival rate is quite high. In an eight-year study by the National Center for Missing and Exploited Children, a not-for-profit organization that works under contract for the United States Department of Justice, only ten out of more than eleven thousand "family" abductions ended in death.

But what if this wasn't a family kidnapping? What if Katie had been abducted by someone else, someone from outside her family? Then the odds got higher that she was dead. Much higher. Of fifteen hundred "non-family" kidnappings in that same eight-year study, 176 children were killed. And those were the ones they knew about. Another 932 kids had disappeared completely.

Besides, time was running out. "You have a two- or three-day period," observed one detective. "After that, statistically, you're looking at someone being killed."

So for purposes of their investigation, police had declared Katie Beers dead. Standard police procedure in an unsolved homicide called for learning everything possible about the victim. Like all detectives, Varrone understood that murder victims usually knew their killer; even if they weren't close, they generally had met somewhere along the line. Murders or kidnappings by strangers did not happen very often—certainly not as frequently as headline writers and movie-of-the-week producers would have the public believe.

The normal starting point for a major investigation, such as a homicide, is the victim's family. Then, in an ever-widening circle, detectives talk to friends, neighbors, and coworkers.

In each interview they try to establish relationships, friendships, patterns of behavior, *anything* that will lead them to the two key facts that usually break a case: Who had motive? Who had opportunity?

When Suffolk detectives began asking questions about Katie Beers, they found some disturbing answers. As the reports came in, almost hourly, Varrone soon discovered that this was no ordinary child of the suburbs. She had been growing up in the underbelly of America, in a substratum of society that most people believed—wrongly—did not exist except in movies like *Deliverance.* Long Island may have had a greater percentage of households earning over fifty thousand dollars a year than anywhere else in the United States, but it still had a not-so-hidden layer of poverty. People on welfare. People without jobs. People in complex dysfunctional families. People like the Beerses and the Inghilleris.

But if the world around Katie was a mess, she was not. She was unusually plucky and shrewd, like Addie Pray, the Tatum O'Neal character in the film *Paper Moon.* She was street smart and tough, but at the same time she was vulnerable and needy. She didn't waste her time on self-pity. Instead, she endured, usually on the strength of her own wits.

In many ways, Katie Beers seemed straight out of a Charles Dickens tale; she was like Little

Nell, Amy Dorrit, Kate Nickleby. She had been oppressed, treated like a servant, by a bizarre string of adults but somehow she managed to thrive, like a daisy squeezing up through a crack in the pavement. She was, in short, a real-life version of Little Orphan Annie. Only she wasn't an orphan. And she had no Daddy Warbucks to save her.

No one went to the hospital with Marilyn Beers when her daughter Katie was born. No one helped her through a long and agonizing labor. No one stayed with her during a difficult postpartum recovery in which she almost came down with toxemia, a condition caused by toxic substances in the blood. And no one took her home from the hospital with her new baby. She went by cab.

Marilyn Beers had no husband. When she found herself pregnant in 1982 at the age of thirty-three, she wasn't even sure who the father was. She had been out drinking one night and met a man in a bar. The next thing she knew she had missed her period.

Marilyn had very little money. She worked long hours as both a cabdriver and a night home-care attendant for an elderly woman. Finding time to care for an infant daughter was not going to be easy. But she never once considered terminating the pregnancy. She didn't believe in abortion. As far as she was concerned, prochoice meant having the baby. That was her choice.

And so Katherine Marie Beers was born in Southside Hospital on Main Street in Bay Shore, Long Island, on December 30, 1982.

When Marilyn and her new daughter were finally released from the hospital, they went directly to 12 Higbie Drive in West Islip, where Marilyn had grown up. The house, just a half block from a busy thoroughfare, looked like a million other tract houses that had sprung up on Long Island during the 1950s and 1960s—a two-story Cape God with a detached garage. Her adoptive parents, Helen and Stuart Beers, had bought the place years earlier, long before Stuart, a Liberty Mutual Insurance Company claims manager, died of emphysema in 1977. Marilyn had continued to live there with her son, John, and her widowed mother.

Growing up had not been easy for Marilyn. Her father didn't cope well; Marilyn got basically what she was to give to Katie: not much. As a child, she was depressed a lot of the time. She dropped out of high school; she had an out-of-wedlock son, Little John, when she was twenty-seven. Today, her brother Robert, forty-one, also adopted, has moved to Connecticut.

They don't see each other much and it doesn't matter, he says. They were never close.

But for many years Robert and his family lived nearby in West Islip. Little John became good friends with his cousin, Jason Beers. They were in the same class in school and sat next to each other in homeroom. They also shared a love of rock music. Sadly, in November 1989, when both boys were thirteen, Jason was killed in an auto accident. His father was taking him and a friend to a Debbie Gibson concert at the Nassau Coliseum when he had a flat tire on a parkway exit ramp. The boys, anxious to get to the concert in time, decided to walk the remaining mile. Jason was hit by a car as he ran across an unlighted section of the four-lane parkway.

When Marilyn got home from Southside Hospital with Katie, she had no baby supplies. A neighbor brought over a used cradle and baby clothes. And sixty-three-year-old Helen Beers did the work—as she had when Little John was born. Marilyn returned to a backbreaking existence of working long hours. A day job. A night job.

She rarely saw Katie. But those were the breaks. She had to work. She wasn't about to go on welfare. She had done that before and she would never do it again, not if she could help it. There was too much hassle and humiliation. She had too much pride.

Helen's heart might have been in the right place but, like her daughter, she was no supermom. When Katie was two months old Marilyn asked her friend, Linda Butler, then twenty-eight and single, if Linda could baby-sit for her. Marilyn said she had a headache and needed to lie down.

"Lie down on my couch," Linda suggested.

"I don't feel comfortable unless I'm at home," Marilyn countered.

So Linda took Katie so that Marilyn could take a nap. The afternoon went by. So did the evening. Marilyn never called. Linda was elated. She had always wanted a baby. This was her chance to at least experiment. She put Katie to bed for the night.

The next day, Marilyn called and asked Linda to keep the child a little while longer. Linda smiled and agreed at once. "A little while longer" turned into a career. Slowly, steadily, Linda became Katie's mom.

Marilyn Beers and Linda Butler met in the mid-seventies when Linda had called for a taxi. When the cab showed up, Marilyn was behind the wheel. They began to chat, and later made plans to get together for coffee. The two were the best of friends ever since.

Marilyn even set Linda up with one of the other drivers she worked with. His name was Sal Inghilleri. He and Linda were the same age, then twenty-nine. And, although Marilyn didn't say it, they seemed physically suited to each other. He wasn't very tall, only five foot six, but he weighed in excess of 250 pounds. Like Linda, he had multiple chins, an enormous girth, and short, pudgy arms.

When Sal was thirteen, his name had appeared in *Newsday,* the Long Island newspaper, as one of five children who were shaken up when their small school bus collided with a car on busy Jericho Turnpike. At the time, the story said, the bus was taking the children to Temple Beth El School in Huntington for special-education classes for brain-injured children.

Linda and Sal began seeing each other, then living together. And then they got married. They moved into a rented house on Myrtle Avenue in West Islip, a few minutes' drive from the Beerses' residence on Higbie Drive. Katie, by then a toddler, went with them. The little girl visited her mother, half brother, and grandmother on weekends but steadily grew to consider "Aunt Lin" and "Uncle Sal" her real parents.

And no wonder. At least Linda and Sal paid *some* attention to her. Back on Higbie Drive it never seemed as if anyone was supervising the little girl. One winter weekend, when she was two, she wandered into the front yard dressed only in a diaper. Breakfast food was smeared all over her face. And all that was between her and the street was a tiny hedge. Neighbors discovered the child and knocked at the door. In the house, no one even realized Katie was gone.

But even though Marilyn was at best a part-time mother, she was unwilling to let Katie go completely. Her mother once asked her why she didn't simply let Linda adopt the child.

"Don't you ever say that again!" Marilyn snapped in a tone so harsh no one ever brought the matter up again.

During the week, Linda took Katie with her everywhere, even when she went to work, maintaining a schedule almost as rigorous as Marilyn's. During the day Linda drove a school bus, and Katie sat right next to her. At other times, Linda cared for a handicapped woman and did a lot of baby-sitting. And Katie was there too. She even went with Linda's mother, Ann Butler, to bingo games.

The next year, when Katie was three, Sal Inghilleri started running into trouble. In September 1987 his driver's license was suspended because he had allowed his auto insurance to lapse. Officially, that meant he couldn't work at any of his various jobs, driving cabs, bakery trucks, and tow trucks. But that didn't stop Sal from driving. He stayed behind the wheel even though he let his driver's license expire altogether in March 1988. He even got a couple of traffic tickets.

What did stop Sal, at least temporarily, was his health. He was overweight and out of shape. In July 1988 he had a heart attack and had to quit working. He and Linda, who by then was bedridden with diabetes, were forced to move in with the Beerses on Higbie Drive. For the first time since she was an infant, Katie was living full-time under the same roof with her mother. Not that it mattered much. Katie frequently slept with Linda, who didn't bother to set an alarm clock. The little girl was often late for school.

It was a squalid existence. The Beers house was a pigsty. It was filled with garbage, infested with roaches and rats, and overrun with countless dogs and as many as twenty-two cats. Many of the dogs and cats weren't housebroken, but no one bothered to clean up the animal feces that were left around. The house smelled of urine. In the yard were boxes and piles of rubbish. At one point, the den ceiling collapsed. And the heater died.

Neither Linda nor Sal did any work around the house. Linda stayed in an upstairs bedroom and communicated via an intercom or by thumping on the floor.

"I need cigarettes!" she would bellow. "Send Katie for cigarettes!"

At age four, Katie had become the family errand girl, at a salary of three dollars a week. She would walk a half block west to busy Udall Road and then another half block south to a strip shopping center that included a deli, a dry cleaner, a florist, a stationery store, a hairdresser, a pizza parlor, and a laundromat. Most mornings she was at Zeigler's Delicatessen when it opened at six-thirty, buying breakfast to take home. At night she was often found at QT Laundromat when it closed at eleven, finishing up a load.

She was quite a sight, with her long blond hair hanging down to her waist the way her mother, Marilyn, wore it. She was never clean. She never wore the right clothes. On cold days she would be in a thin jacket with no hat or gloves. Much of the time she didn't wear shoes. At one point she had a patch on her right cheek from a minor operation; she'd had an infected pimple that had to be removed. At other times she suffered from bad teeth, the reason Linda gave when Katie missed school. As it happened, she missed school a lot.

During the summer Katie was in the long, narrow QT Laundromat twice a day, doing the family wash. The rest of the year, when she was in kindergarten and the first grade, she still went to the laundry three or four times a week. She was so tiny that she had to stand on laundry carts to put her quarters in the industrial-sized Wascomat washing machines.

She had few friends. The neighborhood kids made fun of her because of her messy home. They called her "Dirty Katie" and "The Cockroach Girl." So she hung around the shopping center. The shopkeepers, she discovered, were much nicer.

Katie quickly developed her own circle of grown-up friends. She was in and out of J & B Stationery ten or fifteen times a day. She read the greeting cards, looked at the magazines. She knew the store better than the owner did. And she adored the owner's daughter, Dawn Moody. Starved for affection, Katie told Dawn that she loved her a half-dozen times a day.

Sometimes she would stop by the laundromat to talk to the attendant, Trudy Welsh. One day, as they were chatting, Katie quietly poured herself a cup of coffee from the pot at the front of the shop.

"Katie, you're not old enough to drink coffee," Welsh told the little girl.

Katie shrugged. "I've been drinking coffee since I was four," she replied.

Another regular stop on the Katie tour was Elegant Florists. The owner, Melih Omar Karakas, liked to give her flowers. Sometimes a single red rose, other times a small bouquet of carnations. Now and then Katie would ask for flowers to give to her family or the other shopkeepers—and Karakas would always find some he could spare.

As sweet as she was, Katie Beers was no pushover. She was known throughout the neighborhood for her sharp tongue. "That kid would tell you to go shit in your hat," said one area resident who knew her well. "She was a tough little character."

She called every male she came in contact with "mister." Once a neighbor chided her for going barefoot. "Shut up, *mister*," she retorted. "I know what I'm doing."

When it came to men, Katie wasn't very trusting. At one point that same neighbor, whom she had known for years, offered her a ride and she declined—even though she was lugging home a large pile of laundry. "I don't get in the car with anyone," she replied.

She was particularly careful to make sure no one ever shortchanged her. She knew exactly what she should get back, down to the nickel. No one got away with anything.

"Hey, *mister,*" she said more than once in the shops along the strip. "You gave me the wrong change."

At the same time, neither her mother nor the Inghilleris had any compunction about sending her on errands with less money than she needed. Apparently they were hoping to trade on her special relationship with store owners. This practice came to a head at the local pizzeria, where the burly owner had often given Katie a free slice and a Coke.

The pizzeria owner was a generous man. The many plaques on the dark paneled walls of Howie's Mr. Pizza are testimony to his benevolence. He has been sponsoring West Islip High School football teams for years. But he got angrier every time Katie's extended family phoned ahead for a pizza and sent Katie to pick it up—without enough money to pay for it.

Finally, he said no. "You tell your parents they better send you with the right amount of money," he told the little girl. "I've had it with this."

That apparently touched off a small war with the Inghilleris. That same evening a man called and ordered ten pizzas with various toppings and gave a nonexistent address.

Over the next few weeks the pizza place got several more large orders for pizzas to be delivered to houses that didn't exist. Sal would deny it and there is no way to prove that any of Katie's extended family was behind the fake calls, but everyone who works at Howie's Mr. Pizza will go to their graves believing that Sal Inghilleri was the culprit.

Howie's Mr. Pizza was not the only store that ran into trouble with the Beerses and Inghilleris. In 1990 Katie was sent to a large grocery store in the area without enough money.

Katie and her grandmother, Helen, filled a grocery cart at the Grand Union and pushed it up to the checkout counter. When the cashier tallied the load, it came to more than a hundred dollars. Katie didn't have enough money.

The little girl panicked and ran from the store. She was found later, frightened. Her grandmother wandered outside and sat on a park bench, in a state of confusion and agitation. Grand Union officials tried to question both of them but didn't get any answers. Finally they called the police.

A squad car gathered up Katie and her

grandmother and drove them back to Higbie Drive. The incident would have gone nowhere, but when the cops saw the sordid condition of Katie's home, they contacted Suffolk's Child Protective Services Bureau. A caseworker visited twice.

The second time, however, Linda Inghilleri screamed at the caseworker and chased her away. The woman never returned.

It was the first of many times that the system would fail Katie Beers.

Chapter Seven

IN THE DAYS after Katie disappeared, Marilyn Beers and Linda Inghilleri put up a brave front—on more than one level. The two women may have been friends once but not anymore. In fact, they were in the middle of a protracted—and messy—custody battle over Katie.

But on this day, Tuesday, December 29, they sat side by side at Linda's round kitchen table, chain-smoking Virginia Slims and fielding unending questions from reporters who knocked on the door. It had been less than twenty-four hours since Katie was first reported missing. Other than the message on Linda's answering machine there had been no communication, no ransom demand, no nothing. No one knew what had happened to the little girl. Had she been kidnapped? Did she run away?

"It's sheer hell," Marilyn told one interviewer in her thick Long Island accent. "We just want her back."

To another she gave a plea: "Please, whoever has taken my daughter, please bring her safely back to me," she begged. "Don't hurt Katie."

Linda, meanwhile, used the opportunity to make her case that she was Katie's true mother, not Marilyn. "I toilet trained her. I taught her to talk. I taught her to walk," she said.

At one point, Linda spoke on camera to Katie, hoping against hope that the child had merely run away and was hiding. "I love you and need you," she said. "Please call me or get in touch with me any way you can."

Off camera, though, Marilyn had serious doubts that her daughter was a runaway. "I think somebody forced her out one way or the other," she said. "She's not the kind that would go with just anybody voluntarily."

Linda's mother, Ann Butler, agreed. "Katie is very smart," she said. "If she could have made a phone call like this, she could have gotten away. She had no reason to run away. She knew she could come and go."

Even Sal Inghilleri got into the act. "Our biggest concern is that we find this child well and safe," he told reporters.

To journalists, the principal players in Katie's extended family—Marilyn, Linda, and

Sal—were, as *New York Newsday* columnist Liz Smith put it, "unpalatable." All three were fat and crude, erratic and undereducated, shortsighted and tempestuous.

Had either of the two women possessed a sense of humor, they might have seemed like real-life versions of Roseanne Barr. But they both seemed coarser and more dull witted than that. And they both seemed to be in a perpetual rage, ready to lash out unexpectedly at anything they feared or hated.

For a time, though, they were clever enough to hide their differences from the press. On December 29 few journalists picked up that Marilyn and Linda were at war with each other.

The police, however, were well aware of the continuing feud and had thrown investigators at it full force. What if either Marilyn or Linda had kidnapped the girl to keep the other from getting her?

It didn't seem likely but it wasn't out of the question. Marilyn may have been Katie's natural mother, but Linda had been doing everything she could—including reporting Marilyn to authorities as an unfit mother—to gain custody. It was not a situation the cops could ignore.

Tensions between Marilyn Beers and Linda Inghilleri had begun when they were living together on Higbie Drive in West Islip.

At the time, Marilyn was working two jobs. During the day she was a dispatcher for Town Taxi on Union Boulevard in Bay Shore. At night, she worked another twelve hours—from 8:30 P.M. until 8:30 A.M.—taking care of an elderly woman in Patchogue, a village on Long Island's South Shore. It took her an hour each way to get there and back—using Suffolk County's iffy bus system.

But Marilyn had no choice. In April 1990 she lost her driver's license for more than a year because she had allowed the insurance on her car to lapse. She had no other transportation but the bus.

Early one evening in June 1990 a Suffolk bus pulled up to the entrance of the Long Island Rail Road station in the village of Babylon. Marilyn climbed on and took a seat in the middle. It was around 6:30 P.M.

The bus driver, a woman, was watching her through the rearview mirror.

I know this woman, the driver kept saying to herself. I know this woman.

Finally she turned to Marilyn and asked. "How do I know you?"

"Oh, I'm Marilyn, from Town Taxi."

The driver, Kris Frey, smiled. *Now* she remembered. The previous spring she'd had a friend who was driving for Town Taxi. She had stopped by to see him a few times. Whenever he was off on a run, she would chat with Marilyn and help her locate streets. As a Suffolk County bus driver for six years, Kris knew South Shore streets quite well.

Marilyn moved up to a seat near the front and the two women began to talk. "Normally, I take a later bus," Marilyn explained. "I'm going to my other job."

"You sound like me," Kris laughed. "Two jobs and no husband."

Over the next few months Marilyn rode with Kris almost every evening. Kris talked about her own marital problems. She had just split up with her husband, Martin Frey, and was trying to raise three children—Anthony, then seven, Syndel, five, and William, two—by herself.

Marilyn talked about her own hard life.

"How come you work so much?" Kris asked her on several occasions.

"I got to support the kids and the house and I have a louse of a girlfriend who never contributes a dime," Marilyn would reply, not at all happy.

Marilyn told Kris how much she worried about her kids, John and Katie, but how she was gone all the time, working, and didn't know what to do about it. It was a Catch-22 situation. If she didn't work, she couldn't pay for her kids. But sometimes she felt as if her kids didn't even know her. She resented it. A lot.

Marilyn also resented the bills Sal and Linda were running up. Sal was forever leaning on Helen for money from the one thousand dollars a month she received from her pension and Social Security.

One month the phone alone cost twenty-one hundred dollars. To pay the bill, they got Little John to ask John Esposito for the money. In those days the boy was spending a lot of time with Big John and he immediately came up with the necessary cash.

Most of the calls were to 900-number phone lines—mainly sex and psychics—and, Marilyn contends, were made from the upstairs phone where Linda lay in bed, nursing her diabetes. Linda denied she had made the calls; she blamed them all on Marilyn. But Marilyn was seldom home; only Linda was there when the charges were run up.

Besides, everyone knew Linda lived with a telephone glued to her ear. Whenever Marilyn stopped by Kris's house, she would frequently try to call her home on Higbie Drive. But she rarely was able to get through, even after hours of trying.

There were other bills too. The den ceiling had to be fixed. The heating system was an expensive repair.

As far as Linda and Sal were concerned, any bill run up at 12 Higbie Drive was Marilyn's responsibility. Once Kris stopped by Marilyn's house for coffee and listened in astonishment as Sal took a call from a Sears Roebuck representative. "Look, you'll get your money when you get it," he shouted before slamming down the phone for emphasis.

Sal immediately turned to Marilyn and started yelling.

"Why the hell aren't these bills being paid? I don't understand. You're bringing in all this money. How come these bills aren't being paid?"

Marilyn went into a tantrum herself. "If you gave me some money, the bills *would* be paid," she snapped.

Kris didn't say a word. She knew from all the long conversations with Marilyn that the family finances were a sore point between the Beerses and the Inghilleris. Marilyn had told Kris more than once that she was worried about money. "Mine and my mother's money isn't going far enough," she would say.

In September 1990, Kris came up with an idea to help out both women: she suggested that Marilyn baby-sit for her children. Marilyn promptly took the job, earning a hundred dollars a week to watch Kris's two youngest children—Syndel and William—during the day. Anthony, Kris's seven-year-old, was in school.

For Marilyn, working for Kris meant more than money. It gave her a haven, a place where she could hide from her mounting problems on Higbie Drive.

Kris realized the extent of Marilyn's plight one afternoon that fall. Marilyn had just arrived to watch the children, and Kris explained that she'd decided to give herself a day's vacation from her bus-driving job.

"Marilyn, I'm going to take the day off," Kris told her. "Why don't you go ahead and go home?"

Marilyn didn't respond at first. She seemed uncomfortable. Kris sensed she had touched a raw nerve.

"Go home? What for?" Marilyn finally cried out bitterly. "Little John's in school, and Linda's got Katie wrapped around her little finger. What's to go home for? My daughter doesn't even give a damn about me."

Kris knew that wasn't true. She reminded Marilyn that every time she saw Katie, the little girl was hugging her mother, begging her to stay home from work. "She's always saying, 'Do you have to go, Mom? Can't you stay home today?' " Kris said reassuringly. "Of course she loves you."

But Kris knew there were other things bothering Marilyn. The crowded, messy Higbie Drive house would get to anyone after a while. And then there were the Inghilleris. Kris didn't like Sal, and as for Linda, she had no fondness for her either. She had heard Linda cursing at Sal or the dogs, or bellowing for Katie to bring her cigarettes and snacks. Kris couldn't quite believe the way Linda ran the house—with little Katie as her perpetual servant.

Once Kris summoned up the nerve to ask Marilyn about it.

"Linda sends that little girl to the store alone?" she said. "Marilyn, why don't you send Little John instead? Katie's so young."

Marilyn didn't seem troubled. "Oh, Katie goes all the time," she said with a shrug.

Kris Cosme didn't say more. It wasn't her business, she decided. But she made sure she steered clear of Linda Inghilleri. She had never actually met her—never once did she venture upstairs at 12 Higbie Drive. Yet it seemed to Kris that Linda was determined to cause trouble.

And she did. Kris's biggest battle with Linda centered around a very personal point: Kris's latest boyfriend, who sometimes spent the night. They slept together in Kris's bedroom—the same room where her two-year-old napped in his crib.

Without warning, Linda Inghilleri was on the phone again, calling Suffolk's Child Protective Services to file complaints against Kris. She charged her with being an unfit mother and said Kris was having sex with a man in front of her children.

When the social worker from Child Protective Services showed up at her door, Kris simply laughed. She refused to apologize for seeing men in her own home. She was unabashedly looking for a replacement for her ex-husband, and if that involved sex—and it occasionally did—then so be it. The social worker agreed and she and Kris even became friends.

Later that year, in December 1990, Kris and Marilyn had a falling-out and their friendship crumbled. Just before Christmas, Kris asked Marilyn not to smoke in her house. That led to a minor disagreement concerning the children—so minor, Kris insisted later, that she couldn't remember what it had been about.

But Marilyn didn't forget. The next morning she simply did not show up to take care of Syndel and little William. Nor did she call.

When Kris tried to phone her, she discovered

that the phone in the Higbie Drive house had been disconnected. She tried sending messages through John Esposito—who by this time was playing big brother to her son Anthony as well as to Little John. But still she heard nothing. And so she found another sitter, a former boyfriend who needed a job.

Three months later, Marilyn got on Kris's bus as if nothing had ever happened.

"Where you been?" Kris asked.

"Oh, I've been busy," Marilyn replied. She then began to tell Kris how she needed cash to repair her car. Kris felt sorry for Marilyn and decided to lend her three hundred dollars from an income tax refund she had just received. She didn't know that the plates on the only car registered to Marilyn at that point—a 1974 Dodge sedan—had been suspended.

She never saw Marilyn again.

Marilyn Beers's financial problems continued to worsen. In October 1991 Helen sold the house because banks were about to foreclose on a fifty-thousand-dollar second mortgage, money she got to make repairs but says now she gave to the Inghilleris. In any event, everyone had to move out.

But they didn't. Marilyn and Little John moved into a tiny apartment in what was once the attached garage of a ranch-style house in

Mastic, thirty-five miles east of Bay Shore on the South Shore. It was just about a mile west of Teddy Rodriguez's place.

But the Inghilleris—along with Katie and Helen—stayed. The new owners, an Argentine couple with two young children, had to force them to leave in a protracted court battle. During those months, the new owners said, the Inghilleris trashed the place. "There was no floor. The ceiling was—there was a great hole, one quarter of the living room, where the bathroom upstairs was," said one of the new owners. ". . . They left a truckload of garbage in the house. It was a horror."

The night before she moved, Katie ran barefoot through the backyard to see her next-door neighbor, Cathy Rossi. The woman was surprised to see the child. It was 10:30 P.M. and Katie, who was then eight years old, was shivering in the cold. Rossi gave Katie a hug and a kiss and wished her well.

The next morning the Inghilleris moved into a rented house at 1083 Ocean Avenue in Bay Shore, less than two miles from Higbie Drive. The three-bedroom ranch cost a thousand dollars a month. Helen Beers and Katie went with them.

Downstairs in the mustard yellow house, Linda and Sal rented out an apartment off the books to make some extra cash. Linda also fixed up a room for Katie, with *Beauty and the Beast* posters, a *One Hundred and One Dalmatians* bedspread and curtains, lots of Barbie dolls, stuffed bunnies, and a play vanity.

And for a month or so everything was fine.

Chapter Eight

IN DECEMBER 1991 all hell broke loose. Everything that could go wrong did go wrong. And everything seemed to happen at once.

First there was the problem with Katie's education. The move from Higbie Drive meant that she had changed school districts. She could no longer attend Westbrook Elementary School in West Islip, where she had gone for kindergarten, first, and second grades.

So in the first week of December, Linda Inghilleri took the eight-year-old to Southwest Elementary School in Brentwood to register her for the third grade. But school officials turned her away, politely explaining that Linda was not Katie's legal guardian. Being a godmother apparently cut no ice with the school district.

The rejection did not go over well with Linda.

She started yelling and swearing and finally stormed out.

A week or so later Marilyn Beers visited the elementary school herself. She brought a notarized statement saying that she suffered financial hardship and was, therefore, assigning custodial control over Katie to Linda Inghilleri. In addition, the document stated that Marilyn planned to give her friend permanent custody over the child.

School officials were still not satisfied. They again refused to enroll little Katie.

Marilyn did not take the turndown lightly. In fact, she made Linda's previous outburst seem calm and reasoned. She threw a radio and yelled a racial epithet. After she left, the school summoned the police.

But Linda moved first. She called Suffolk's Child Protective Services, lodging a formal complaint against the school. She accused Southwest officials of neglecting Katie and apparently the Child Protective Services Bureau agreed. On January 13, 1992, a caseworker contacted the school and convinced the principal to register the child.

But next to the other problems in Katie's life, the flap at Southwest Elementary seems minor. As events were playing out at the school, Linda's diabetes started acting up. Gangrene was developing in her left leg and she had to be admitted to a local hospital. Katie remained at the yellow ranch house on Ocean Avenue with Helen Beers and Sal Inghilleri.

She was clearly a troubled little girl. On December 5 she demonstrated the depth of her pain. That afternoon she stepped out the back door and calmly walked across the yard with a full ashtray. Next door, her new neighbor, Joan Bergo, was outside on her deck watching.

Katie carefully emptied the ashtray on the dry, high grass, took out a cigarette lighter and set fire to the lawn. Then she turned and walked deliberately into the house as flames began shooting up behind her.

Bergo screamed at the girl, "What are you doing! Fire! Fire!"

But Katie never even turned her head.

Bergo rushed to her front yard, where her husband, Harry, was raking leaves.

"Harry, there's a fire next door," she shouted.

"Don't be silly," Harry responded.

"I'm not kidding!"

Harry and some other neighbors tried to put out the blaze with garden hoses but the flames spread too quickly. Joan Bergo ran into her house and called the fire department.

Fire fighters raced to the scene, their sirens screaming, and arrived ten minutes after the fire started. They put it out quickly, before it could spread. And since it didn't cause any significant property damage, the fire captain was willing to list the blaze as a "fire of unknown origin."

By the time the fire engines left, a huge crowd had formed. But Katie never came outside.

Neighbors such as the Bergos believe she may have set the fire because she was upset at leaving her childhood home and moving into a new neighborhood. They also speculate that Katie was angry at having been left alone with Sal and Helen while Linda was in the hospital.

Apparently there was more to it than that. The previous April, while the two families were still living together on Higbie Drive, Sal allegedly had sexually molested Katie Beers.

At the time, however, Katie did not tell anyone about the incident for months. She kept it bottled up inside. But with Linda in the hospital and her aging grandmother Helen barely a footnote in the Inghilleri household, Katie began to grow fearful of Sal.

She started talking about the incident obliquely. At first she made derogatory comments about Sal to anyone who would listen. Then she started telling people that she hated Sal, that she was afraid of him. "If he ever comes near me again or hurts me again, I'm going to get a kitchen knife and kill him," she told Kris Cosme's son, Anthony.

After a while she could no longer keep her dreadful secret to herself. On a weekend visit to her mother and half brother at their new home in Mastic, she told Little John and a friend of his what Sal had done.

"She just said it," Little John said later. "I didn't say nothin' about it at first."

But a few weeks later, Little John told Marilyn. "I thought she had the right to know," he said.

Marilyn did not hesitate. On January 14, 1992, she and Teddy Rodriguez went straight to the Inghilleri home on Ocean Avenue. Marilyn began packing Katie's and Helen's things, throwing them into whatever bags she could find. Linda, back from the hospital but unable to move around, kept yelling from her bedroom for Marilyn to stop.

So did Katie. Just because she hated and feared Sal didn't mean she wanted to leave Linda. She started screaming and crying and grabbed on to Linda's round kitchen table, refusing to let go.

Linda called 911.

A police officer came to the house, hoping to make peace by trying to convince Marilyn to let the child stay. Marilyn was stubborn. She wanted her daughter. Finally she announced that she was going to file sex abuse charges against Sal. The officer relented.

It was a surprise announcement, the first Linda had ever heard of the charges. Katie promptly denied them, claiming Little John had forced her to make up a story about sex abuse because he hated Sal himself. Sal, it seems, was something of a disciplinarian. He had clipped Little John's wings when the two families were living together on Higbie Drive, and Little John resented it.

But Marilyn was determined to get her daughter away from Sal Inghilleri. She ignored Katie's entreaties and moved the child into the garage apartment in Mastic Beach. Helen went too. It was a tight squeeze, the four of them crowded into a one-bedroom apartment. Little John slept on a convertible sofa in the living room, although he rarely bothered to pull out the mattress. In the bedroom, Helen had one of the two single beds. And Marilyn and Katie shared the other one. Given Marilyn's girth it was a tight squeeze indeed.

Marilyn was true to her word. She immediately filed a complaint against Sal Inghilleri with the sex crimes unit of the Suffolk County police. Although they took their time about it, detectives eventually investigated. On October 16, 1992, just two months before Katie disappeared, Sal was arrested and formally arraigned on one count of first degree sexual abuse in First District Court in Hauppauge. At the same time, the Suffolk County district attorney's office obtained an order of protection on Katie's behalf. Sal was officially barred from being alone with her for one year.

It wasn't surprising, therefore, that on December 29 the Suffolk County police kidnapping task force thought it had a suspect in Sal Inghilleri. He had been formally charged with sexually abusing the missing girl. Police sources said he had confessed, admitting to the abuse. "We know what he did because Sal told us in his own words what he did," one of the cops involved told a reporter for *Newsday*.

Suddenly the reporters knocking on the door of 1083 Ocean Avenue didn't want to talk to Linda or Marilyn anymore. They wanted Sal.

Linda refused to let the journalists inside. She was sick of reporters and her family backed her up. "Let him take his business over to his mother's," one of her sisters suggested.

So Sal stood outside on the porch or, when it started raining, sat in the front seat of his incredibly messy car, giving interviews.

He denied that he had anything to do with Katie's disappearance. "I can account for every move I made up until ten-thirty Monday night," he said. He also denied that he had sexually abused Katie—or that he had signed a confession. "I'm very confident that I'll be vindicated of these charges," he said. "I never touched her. I never touched that girl." He pulled off his sunglasses and pointed to Lulu, a Pomeranian standing in the yard. "The only one I ever touched was that dog. What am I going to do with a little girl? People are sick."

Sal maintained that Marilyn had had two motives in mind when she came storming into the Ocean Avenue house that January afternoon—eleven months before to remove Helen and Katie—and neither had anything to do with sexual abuse.

Marilyn took her mother, he said, because she wanted access to the elderly woman's pension. And she seized her daughter because she was jealous of Linda's hold over the girl. It was Marilyn who convinced Katie to contrive the charges, he argued, because she wanted complete custody of her daughter. No court would ever allow Katie to live in the home of a child molester.

The sex abuse charges against Sal Inghilleri in the winter of 1992 should have ended the Beers-Inghilleri alliance right there. But Katie began pestering her mother, begging to visit Aunt Lin on the weekends. She whined and cried, wheedled and nagged. And eventually Marilyn recanted. She allowed Katie to go the Inghilleris on Fridays, if she returned in time for school.

Marilyn's decision to let Katie visit the Inghilleris seems even more remarkable given Linda's actions at the time. She was actively trying to regain custody of the child, although her methods seem misguided. Instead of going to court, she repeatedly complained to the Suffolk County Child Protection Services Bureau that Marilyn was an unfit mother who was neglecting her daughter.

She had plenty of grounds. Marilyn's rented garage apartment continued to be crowded, ill-kempt, filthy, and foul. But it was a little like the pot calling the kettle black. The Inghilleris were not endearing themselves to their new neighbors in Bay Shore that spring. Almost as soon as they moved in, Sal began towing junked cars and campers to the backyard, using them for parts. Every time there was a new one, the Bergos next door would joke bitterly to themselves that one of the cars had had a baby.

Sal also filled the yard with old refrigerators, some with the doors left on. Grass grew high around the wreckage. One neighbor built a fence to avoid having to see the mess.

Area residents began complaining to the town of Islip and finally their pleas paid off. Sal got rid of the junk, but the yard remained unmowed, unattractive—and distinctly unsuburban.

Neighbors had other problems with the Inghilleris. Every morning around nine or nine-thirty Linda would start screaming at Sal or her two black-and-tan Pomeranians, Lulu and Kiki.

Several times that spring, neighbors complained to Sal about Linda's screaming. One day Harry Bergo stopped Sal on the front lawn.

"Sal, can I talk to you a minute?" he said. "Look, I have grandchildren. I don't like them hearing that kind of language. They'll be picking it up."

"Talk to her mother," Sal responded. "She has more influence."

So Joan Bergo tried discussing the problem with Linda's mother, Ann Butler.

She was unresponsive. "If you don't like it, build a fence," Ann snapped. "You're a nosy neighbor. Stop calling the town."

Sometime in the late spring, Linda's battle with diabetes grew more serious. Gangrene had spread, and doctors were forced to remove her left leg.

With school out, Katie started staying with the Inghilleris more and more often. Marilyn allowed the stepped-up visits in part because she knew Linda, now in a wheelchair, needed the help. But she had been led to believe that Linda and Sal were splitting up. With Sal out of the picture, there was no danger of his molesting her daughter again.

Sal, though, was very much in the picture.

Any "separation" between him and Linda was apparently a device, a guise so that the couple could collect more disability for her leg.

Katie spent all of August 1992 with the Inghilleris. It was a strange new world for Katie; for the first time she had other little girls to play with, but she didn't always play well with the other children. She was overly possessive of her toys. At the aboveground pool of Harry and Joan Bergo next door she was not always the perfect guest. On several occasions, while the other kids took turns walking the Bergos' granddaughter, Shayna, then four, across the pool, Katie refused.

Katie also took a lot of teasing from neighborhood kids for setting the fire the previous December.

"You set a fire," the kids would chant. "Katie set a fire."

Katie denied it. "I did not," she'd snap back. "Did *not!*."

One day Joan Bergo pulled the child aside. She'd wanted to talk to Katie alone for many months.

"Why did you start that fire, Katie?" she asked.

"I didn't," Katie said quickly. "I emptied the ashtray."

"Katie," Bergo said gently but firmly, "I hollered fire and you never turned around to look back. That was not an accident."

Katie shrugged. She changed the subject and walked away. It was none of Joan Bergo's business.

The following month, Katie returned to Mastic and entered the fourth grade at Tangier Smith Elementary School. But within six weeks she'd been sent home with head lice.

Marilyn cut her waist-length hair and sent her back to school, but officials found more lice and sent Katie home again. The little girl never returned, and by late November or early December, officials at Tangier Smith had filed an educational neglect charge against Marilyn Beers, starting a Child Protective Services investigation.

At the same time Marilyn had decided to cut Linda Inghilleri off from the child. Katie was no longer making weekend trips to Bay Shore, and Linda was upset. In mid-December, just a week before Katie disappeared, Linda showed up at the Beers' apartment in Mastic. But Marilyn wasn't there and Katie was in bed, sick. Linda left empty-handed. "Tell your fucking mother she's not going to sleep a good night's sleep when I get through with her," she told Little John. "If it's the last thing I'll dò, she'll never see Katie."

What Inghilleri meant, she said later, was that she was going to have Suffolk Child Protective Services check in on the child. She feared for Katie's safety.

A few days later Linda's mother, Ann Butler, made the trip to Mastic. She found Marilyn and they had a long talk. Apparently Ann Butler was less antagonistic than her daughter, because Marilyn agreed to let Katie visit Linda in Bay Shore for four days between Christmas and New Year's.

It was around this time that Katie began to wear her large floppy black hat constantly, practically sleeping in it. It was also the time that she decided to change her name. No more was she to be called Katie Beers. Indeed, she wanted nothing to do with the old Katie Beers. She was to be known as Katherine. It seemed to be her way of gaining some control over her life. With a new name would come a new identity. And maybe a new life. But no one—not her mother, not her godmother—paid the least bit of attention.

Chapter Nine

SAL INGHILLERI may have been a suspect in Katie Beers's disappearance, and he certainly made for colorful copy. Even the *New York Times* did a story on him. But he was hardly number one on anyone's list of suspects. That designation fell to John Esposito.

Everyone knew it, including Big John. It would have been hard for him not to know. He was under twenty-four-hour-a-day surveillance. Wherever he went, a team of detectives went with him. They put him to bed at night; they saw him first thing in the morning. They followed him to his brother Ron's house in Selden and to his lawyer's offices in Bay Shore. They even walked up and down the aisles of the supermarket with him. It was, Lieutenant Dominick Varrone freely admitted at the time, "a campaign of intimidation."

Esposito decided to fight back. On December 30, the second day of Katie's disappearance, he called his attorney, Sidney Siben.

"I want to tell the public my side of the story," he told Siben.

The lawyer warned his client that a press conference might get dicey, given Esposito's previous encounter with the law. But Esposito was confident. If he told everything that happened, maybe the cops would see that he was innocent and leave him alone.

Siben decided Esposito might be right. A good offense could turn into a good defense. So Siben called a press conference for that morning in the second-floor library of his law firm on Main Street in Bay Shore. He sat on one side of Esposito, and his nephew and law partner, Andrew Siben, sat on the other.

Esposito started to cry almost immediately. "Just find the girl, for God's sake," he whispered. "I'll be honest with you, she likes to sit on my lap and steer the car. . . . I want to do everything I can to find her."

He told the reporters the same story he told the cops. He said that he and Katie had bought a *Home Alone 2* video game at Toys "Я" Us and brought it back to his house to try out. After that, they went to Spaceplex. "The last time I seen her is when I gave her the five dollars and she was walking towards the machines," he said in front of the cameras. "Then after a while I started getting scared. Where is she?"

One of the reporters asked him about Katie's phone message. "If you heard the tape," Big John said, tears streaming down his cheeks, "you'd know it was her. She said, 'Somebody kidnapped me, a man, a man with a knife kidnapped me.' "

Sidney Siben immediately interrupted. "If it was him," he said, pointing at Esposito, "she'd say, '*John* kidnapped me.' "

Esposito nodded in agreement.

Andrew Siben decided this was a good time to make another point in Esposito's favor. He held up a Troll doll that Katie had named Big John and given to Esposito for Christmas. With it was a card bearing a message written with a green felt-tip pen: "Thanks for being like a big brother to me."

Things seemed to be going well. Then reporters asked about Esposito's arrest in 1977. Andrew Siben promptly cut them off. He said there would be no comment on the earlier case, that it was long ago over, that it had been sealed and that it had no bearing on the disappearance of Katie Beers.

Afterwards, reporters rushed to Linda Inghilleri's house for reaction. Marilyn Beers was there too.

"I'm going crazy," Marilyn said in her thick Long Island accent. "Every time the phone rings, we all jump."

Like Esposito, both Marilyn and Linda had a

hard time keeping in the tears. It was, Marilyn noted, her daughter's tenth birthday.

"I want my baby back!" she sobbed. "I know it is not like Katie to just run off."

Both women said they were suspicious of Esposito because of something he told Linda the night that Katie disappeared.

While speaking on the phone from Spaceplex, he had said that little Katie had taken off her coat and black floppy blossom hat while she was still in his pickup truck. Linda didn't believe him and said so, calling Esposito a liar over the phone. "She loved that hat," she told reporters. "She never took it off."

Linda had other reasons for suspecting Esposito. She had given Katie some letters to mail when she left with Big John on December 28. But when she asked Esposito about them over the phone, he had responded, "What letters?" It may have seemed small, but to Linda it meant Esposito was lying about something.

Others were suspicious of John Esposito as well. At headquarters of Big Brothers/Big Sisters of Suffolk Inc. in Hauppauge, executive director Paul Freedman had been reading the stories of Katie's disappearance in the Long Island edition of *Newsday*. When he spotted Esposito's name, he sat up straight.

"This is the guy," he thought. He immediately drove to the Fourth Precinct headquarters, also in Hauppauge, where Detective Dominick Varrone was running the investigation in the basement.

Freedman told detectives of Esposito's history with Big Brothers, how all the information the group had gathered on him had been placed in a file marked CONCERNED. He showed them the records. He wished he had more.

I wish we had done a psychological profile on him, he thought as he pulled out of the Fourth Precinct's parking lot several hours later. It would have been good for the police. They'd have had an incredible profile of a fixated pedophile.

As it happened, the police already had a general profile of pedophiles on hand. It had been prepared some time ago by the behavioral sciences unit at the FBI Academy in Quantico, Virginia, the section made famous by the novel and movie *The Silence of the Lambs.* Psychologists generally divide pedophiles into two categories. *Fixated pedophiles* have never progressed to having relationships with people their own age. Instead, they become sexually interested in children, usually of the same sex as themselves. Their sexual interest continues for years. *Regressed pedophiles* have adult sexual relationships. But sometimes, generally under the influence of drugs or alcohol, they have an incestuous encounter with a child. Normally the number of episodes is very few.

The detectives looked very carefully at the

information that Freedman provided. They already thought Esposito was their man. This only convinced them further. Now they wanted to know everything they could find out about John Esposito, especially how to break him.

John Esposito's character—indeed his very life—was no doubt profoundly influenced by a tragedy that took place during World War II, years before he was born. His brother Ralph Junior had been playing in the yard when an ice cream truck came by. The five-year-old ran after it. A passing car slammed him into a tree and he died instantly. It was his mother Rose's birthday.

After that, Rose Esposito became very protective of her children, a trait that lasted all her life. Until the day she died in 1991, she would not go to bed until she was sure her four sons—by then grown men—had made it home for the evening. Each had to check in so that she could get a decent night's sleep.

A few years after she lost Ralph Junior, Rose and her husband, Ralph Senior had a second son, William. Then, in 1948, Rose got pregnant for a third time. On May 14, 1949, she went into labor and gave birth to a healthy boy, Ronald. Then, surprising everyone present, her labor continued. Unbeknownst to her obstetrician, she had been carrying fraternal twins.

And so John Esposito was born, coming into the world at a scant three pounds. No one expected him to make it, least of all Rose and Ralph Esposito. But Rose gave the child special attention. Already predisposed to smother children with love and protection, she lavished even more care and kindness on her sickly son, John. She never let up, even after he began to grow healthy and strong. She doted on John and he, in turn, was the proverbial mama's boy, running her errands, staying close to home.

Another son, Patrick, was born when the twins were five, and the family moved to a two-story house in Bay Shore in what was then a semirural area of woods and streams. It seemed like the perfect place for boys to grow up; they could build forts in the woods, fish for trout, ride their bikes on dirt roads. If those pleasures weren't enough to keep her sons nearby, Rose made the place even more of a boys' paradise. There was a tree house in the backyard where they could spend the night and a 1952 Chevy that they could drive around the backyard in circles. With toys like that, the other kids in the neighborhood were always at the Espositos'. "Aunt Rose" encouraged the visits; all the more reason for her sons to stay at home.

As the area developed, the Espositos' street, North Saxon Avenue between Sunrise Highway and Southern State Parkway, became a busy thoroughfare. Speeding cars on the roadway brought back the painful memory of the son that Rose Esposito had lost. For years her children watched as she yelled at motorists who drove too fast. Sometimes she was brought to tears.

The other Esposito sons managed to grow up normally despite their overly protective mother. While his twin brother, Ron, was a guy's guy, tough and boisterous, John seemed a bit weak. As a youngster, he covered his face when he heard other boys testing out newly learned swear words. By the time he and Ron dropped out of high school in the eleventh grade, he had stopped hanging out with kids his age, preferring the friends of his younger brother, Patrick. Since he was old enough to drive, he could take them to the movies, the shopping malls, or the local auto races.

He may have gone out with a few girls in his teens but dates of that sort had ended by the time he was twenty. He stayed at home mostly, with his parents and brothers. He built a basketball court and a swimming pool. The yard was always filled with children.

In 1969 Ron enlisted in the marines and went to Vietnam. John made no macho moves like that. Instead, he waited until he received his

Selective Service notice, but he was never drafted. He flunked the physical. "He really felt bad about that," his sister-in-law Joyce recalled.

As the twins grew up, both Ron and John had worked off and on for their father, who had developed a carpet-laying business. When they dropped out of high school, they both got jobs with a building contractor who lived in the neighborhood.

They were each natural carpenters and John developed a subspecialty in detail work. They became particularly good at building home extensions, putting up decks, and doing renovations. Eventually they formed their own company, J & R Home Improvements of Bay Shore.

If John had any weaknesses as a carpenter it was his inability to withstand pressure. Whenever a job had a tight deadline, John would back out, claiming his heart was bothering him. Sometimes he got his mother to call contractors to tell them he was sick and they would have to get someone else. This trait was ultimately to prove his undoing in the cat-and-mouse game he was playing with the Suffolk P.D.

That night on television the story of Katie Beers was again at the top of the local news. Her picture, taken at her elementary school, was again broadcast into millions of homes throughout the New York metropolitan area. This time there was also a picture of Katie taken just three days earlier at her birthday party at Linda Inghilleri's. She was wearing her floppy hat.

The newscasters all noted, with grim sadness in their voices, that this day, December 30, had been Katie's tenth birthday. But the bulk of the news reports that night were about John Esposito. In each case he was filmed sitting in front of shelves of lawbooks, his face contorted with pain as he wept over the disappearance of Katie Beers. He explained over and over that he didn't know what had become of her. He'd lost sight of her for a while, and she was gone.

The TV news that night also carried sound bites of Marilyn Beers and Linda Inghilleri talking about Katie, hoping for her return.

The birthday girl saw it all. She inched her way forward on the dirty mattress and pressed her face to the television set. Each time her mother or godmother appeared, she kissed their pictures, her own tears smudging the screen.

Chapter Ten

THE OPERATION had all the earmarks of a hastily conceived military campaign. First, detectives knocked gingerly on the door of District Court Judge Steven Lotto at 4:30 A.M. They asked him to get out of bed to sign search warrants for the property at 1416 North Saxon Avenue in Bay Shore. Specifically, they wanted to examine the main house, the converted garage, three sheds, and an aboveground swimming pool. In other words, everything.

Then the cops arrived at the Esposito compound in full force. It was, in essence, a surprise raid. By 8:00 A.M. a team of seven detectives was going over everything. They ploughed through every drawer. They examined every closet. They raked through piles of leaves. They scrutinized every piece of paper in his office. They sifted through his linen, dirty and clean. "They ransacked the place," Esposito complained. "They took it apart piece by piece like they were looking for a body."

In fact, that was *exactly* what they were doing. And if they didn't find a body, they were also searching for anything they could find that could lead them to one. To little Katie Beers.

Despite his complaints, Esposito offered no resistance. Indeed, he was extremely cooperative, politely opening doors and giving directions. If there were any problems at all, it came from the dogs. Esposito owned a beagle named Brutus who bayed at the cops as they wandered around the property. There were also two German shepherds on hand, dogs belonging to Esposito's sister-in-law Joan. She was on a Christmas vacation in Mexico at the time and Esposito was caring for the animals while she was away. But, despite some inopportune growling, they weren't a serious problem.

Joan had lived in the main house until two months earlier. The widow of John's brother Patrick, she had decided she didn't want the pain of living there any longer. When she moved, John became the last Esposito left at 1416 North Saxon Avenue. Part of the main house was rented; the rest remained vacant.

By 10:00 A.M., the cops had completed their search. They hadn't found Katie Beers. They hadn't found anything that would lead them to Katie Beers. But they hadn't exactly come away empty, either.

When an investigator opened a garbage pail outside the house, he discovered two wet sheets that had been stained. Was it blood? It was hard to tell. The sheets went straight to the FBI for analysis. In Esposito's office, just off the kitchen, were some printed instructions for a tape recorder. But the detectives couldn't find the tape recorder itself, which seemed strange. When they asked Esposito what happened to it, he said he didn't know.

Finally, police found some items that actually bolstered Esposito's story. There was the *Home Alone 2* Nintendo game he said he had bought with Katie—and a receipt from Toys "Я" Us showing that he had gotten it on Monday afternoon.

The police didn't tell Esposito at the time, but the 7-Eleven where he and Katie had stopped that afternoon had no less than six video cameras from the Dictograph Security Company mounted into the ceiling. One of them had taped Katie that afternoon while she paid for her Slurpee. To a limited extent, that helped confirm Esposito's story. But it didn't exonerate him. Katie had put her change back into her pocketbook carefully and deliberately. The detectives could readily see that this was a child who watched her money, who did not allow herself to be shortchanged. Someone like that did not leave her purse lying around on a shelf while she went to an indoor amusement park before going home.

In the same videotape, John Esposito could be seen standing at Katie's side.

Even though some of Esposito's story was checking out, the police were not about to let him off the hook. There were still plenty of holes in his version of events. The biggest gap—the one you could drive a truck through—was that no one, except John Esposito, had actually seen Katie Beers at Spaceplex. "It could be that no one remembers seeing her because there were hundreds of children there," one detective said. "Or maybe she was never there at all."

A little later that day, Esposito took a call from a reporter. He said he wasn't angry at the police for focusing on him. "I guess they have to do everything they can to find her," he said. "I don't blame them, really. I just want to find her, too. The longer it goes by, the scarier it gets. I hope they find her alive."

John Esposito was a friendly man, a gentle man. Everyone who met him seemed to like him—even the cops assigned to tail him. So it was no surprise that, in 1970, he was given immediate approval for membership in the Big Brothers, an organization that was then being run by Catholic Charities. The group put him in touch with William Umlauft, an eight-year-old boy, one of six children whose father had died.

The first thing John did was to ask William if he wanted to go for a ride in his shiny new truck. Did he! The boy was thrilled. After that, John saw William regularly, taking him bowling or to Mets baseball games in New York City. He also showered the boy with gifts. A bike for his birthday. A toy truck. A TV set.

But then Umlauft started to get older. By 1977 John had outgrown this "little brother." One day he went to the Sunrise Mall, a shopping center in Massapequa, Long Island, about twenty-five miles west of Bay Shore. While there, he met a seven-year-old boy outside a pet store. He tried to lead the child away, but the boy started crying loudly. Security guards were nearby and John fled. A month or so later the guards saw Esposito at the mall again and called the police. He was arrested.

Esposito's attorney, Sidney Siben, worked out a plea bargain with prosecutors and John pleaded guilty in a Nassau County court to unlawful imprisonment, a misdemeanor. He was put on probation and court records were sealed because a juvenile was involved. Esposito told Nassau County police he was looking for a friend.

At the time Big Brothers did not do thorough background checks and the organization didn't learn of his arrest and conviction. Esposito was assigned another "little brother," this one a seven-year-old whose parents were in the middle of a messy divorce.

Unfortunately for Esposito, the boy moved to Florida with his mother in the early eighties. It was a double blow for John; his father, Ralph Senior, died around that time. The eternal child had lost both his father and his friend. He was getting older whether he wanted to or not.

This time Esposito turned to his family to find someone. Joan Esposito, the new wife of his younger brother Patrick, had grown up in West Islip, not far from the Beers house on Higbie Drive. She knew Marilyn Beers. Rose Esposito too had met Marilyn when she had ridden in her cab.

Joanie told Esposito that Marilyn was unmarried and struggling to raise two children, a one-year-old daughter named Katie and a seven-year-old son called John. Esposito promptly volunteered to help out with the boy, who soon became known as Little John.

Esposito followed the same pattern with Little John as he had with his previous "little brothers." He was like a godsend to Little John, who had been largely ignored by his mother. He lavished gifts on him—an eleven-hundred-dollar stereo for Christmas—and he took the little boy to places he could only dream about. That summer, the summer of 1985, he treated Little John, then seven, to a trip to Orlando, Florida, to visit Disney World. Accompanying them were Esposito's twin brother, Ron, Ron's wife, Joyce, and their three young children.

Not everyone was happy about John Esposito's involvement with Little John. One day Teddy Rodriguez, Little John's father, stopped by the Beers house on Higbie Drive to visit Marilyn. While Teddy was there, Big John arrived to pick up Little John for one of their regular Sunday outings.

Marilyn introduced them. "This is John," she said. "He's Johnny's big brother."

Esposito and Rodriguez shook hands and chatted awhile. As soon as the two Johns left, Teddy began asking Marilyn questions.

"Is he married?"

"No."

"That guy is either gay or he's a fem," Teddy asserted immediately. "You better watch it with him and Johnny. There could be something. I don't like to judge people, the way they act and all, but you should watch it."

Marilyn would hear none of it. "He's a friend of the family," she said. "Nothing's going on."

In March 1988, Esposito decided he wanted a second "little brother." He applied to Big Brothers/Big Sisters of Suffolk to be a mentor. This was a different organization than the one run by Catholic Charities and standards were far more rigorous. Esposito was required to attend an hour-long orientation session in a conference room with about ten other would-be mentors. He filled out a four-page application, and learned that applicants must go through an exacting screening process.

The social worker in charge explained that there would be a three-hour interview, a personality profile test, references, and a police check to see if the applicant had any record. Esposito also learned that of the ten people who were interested in joining, only one or two would probably be chosen.

A few weeks later, on April 8, Esposito wrote, by hand, a letter to Big Brothers. In it he said that his twin brother, Ron, had given police his name in 1977 when he was arrested for an unspecified crime in Nassau County and that the charge might not have been removed from

Esposito's record. "Please tell me if I am able to volunteer or not?" he asked.

Paul Freedman, the executive director of Big Brothers/Big Sisters of Suffolk, felt the letter was contrived and showed dishonesty. Five days later, on April 13, 1988, he replied to Esposito by mail:

> Dear Mr. Esposito:
>
> I am in receipt of your letter of April 8, 1988. With respect to the circumstances you describe, we feel it would be best not to continue with your application process.
>
> Thank you for the interest you expressed in Big Brothers/Big Sisters of Suffolk, and good luck in your future endeavors.

Freedman placed copies of both letters in John Esposito's file. And then he added Esposito's name to what is known in the organization as "the concerned list"—people Big Brothers doesn't trust.

Two years later, around January 1990, Freedman got a call from a former big brother who said he had seen an index card hanging in a Bay Shore supermarket from a man who said he was a "Long Island *Big Brother*" for over ten years. He would volunteer his time for a boy who "needs a man in his life," and provided instructions for how to reach him. He described himself as a "person of good character" that could be trusted and respected. The card was signed, "John Esposito."

Freedman sent one of his employees to the supermarket to get the card. A few months later, someone else found a similar ad in the local *Pennysaver*. The ad had been first placed in December 1989, although the Big Brothers didn't learn of it for a few months—until after it discovered the index cards.

> DOES YOUR SON NEED a man in his life, a friend who cares and is trusting. Call JOHN A BIG BROTHER who is doing it on his own. Call after 7:00.

Freedman called the sex crimes unit of the Suffolk County police. He was told that the writer of the ads had not broken any laws. But Freedman was also advised to contact families using the program to warn them.

He drafted a letter that he now sends to all parents awaiting assignment of a big brother. It reads:

> Dear Parent:
>
> Our agency is very concerned about not

Little Katie Beers in her fourth-grade school picture. (PAUL DEMARIA, COURTESY OF THE NEW YORK *DAILY NEWS*)

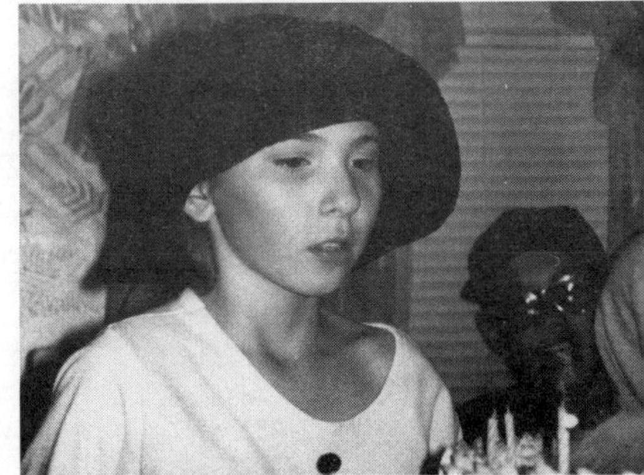

Katie at her tenth birthday party, just days before she was abducted. (COURTESY OF MARY MCLOUGHLIN, © *NEW YORK POST*)

John Esposito being led out of the Fourth Precinct to his arraignment. (MARY MCLOUGHLIN, © *NEW YORK POST*)

John Esposito's Bay Shore, Long Island house. (Maria Eftimiades)

The converted garage behind Esposito's house where the bunker was located. (Maria Eftimiades)

The six-by-seven-foot dungeon where Katie Beers was held captive for 16 days.
(WILLIE ANDERSON, THE NEW YORK *DAILY NEWS*)

Katie Beers leaves the Fourth Precinct with a social worker just hours after her release.
(BILL TURNBULL, THE NEW YORK *DAILY NEWS*)

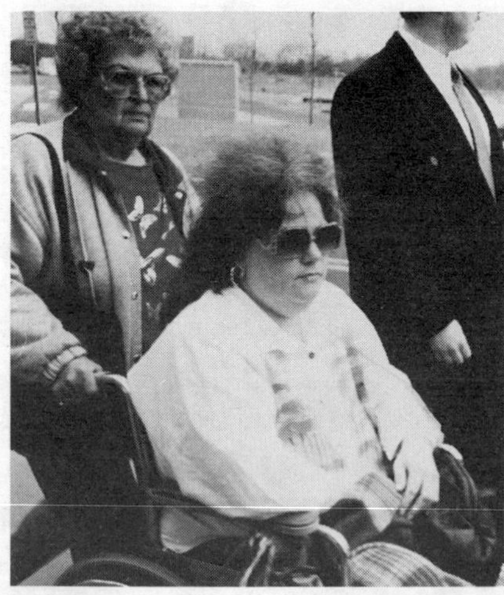

Linda Inghilleri, Katie's godmother, plans to fight for custody. (MARIA EFTIMIADES)

Sal Inghilleri, Linda's husband, faces trial for the alleged sexual abuse of Katie. (KIMBERLY BUTLER)

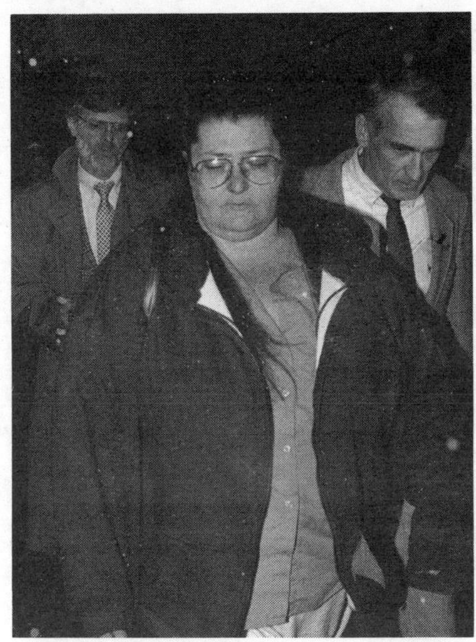

Marilyn Beers denies allegations that she's an unfit parent. (JOHN ROCA, THE NEW YORK *DAILY NEWS*)

Marilyn Beers lives in the converted garage of this Mastic Beach ranch house. (MARIA EFTIMIADES)

Little John, Katie's half brother, alleges that John Esposito sexually molested him for years. (MARIA EFTIMIADES)

Katie now attends Springs School in East Hampton, Long Island. (MARIA EFTIMIADES)

being able to service your child and understand some of you may be feeling overwhelmed and even desperate.

It has been brought to our attention that some people are taking advantage of your dilemma and may in fact do harm to your child.

Here is an example posted on the community service bulletin board in a supermarket and in a *Pennysaver* ad.

[The entire bulletin board ad was included here.]

Before you answer one of these ads or even [if you] have a question about other volunteer organizations please call our agency. Appropriate screening and training is essential in protecting your child from people who don't have your child's best interest at heart.

We are also offering training for parents and their children with information and personal safety tips, so your children can be better protected.

For more information call me at [*phone number*].

The police campaign of intimidation did not let up on John Esposito following the search of the Esposito compound on the day of New

Year's Eve. Since a wooden gate blocked the view of police sitting in the street, officers were posted in the main house so that they could watch Esposito's comings and goings from his quarters in the remodeled garage. Cops could also be seen in neighbors' yards on either side and to the rear.

Esposito tried to keep his composure, fighting back in subtle ways. Sometimes he would stop by the unmarked car in front of the Esposito property and give the cops inside a written itinerary. By all accounts he always was very friendly.

"This is where I'm going to be, guys," he would say.

Other times he was more up-front about his desires. "When are you guys leaving?" he would ask. "When are you guys leaving?"

At night, Esposito seldom went out. Sometimes he ordered in dinner, usually a pizza.

When detectives changed shifts each evening, the night crew would be filled in on where he had been all day.

"He went to his brother's, to the supermarket, to the lawyers," the day detectives might say.

"Where is he now?"

"Inside."

"When did he go to sleep?"

No one ever knew. The curtains were always drawn. It was impossible to tell what Esposito was doing at night. Or, for that matter, what he was doing with the food he had purchased in the grocery store or ordered from the pizzeria.

Chapter Eleven

WITH THE SPOTLIGHT on John Esposito, the police tried a different tack. On New Year's Day, a team of cops went to the intersection of Route 347 and Southern Boulevard in Nesconset, formed search parties, and spread out.

At first, it seemed like an improbable place to find anything connected to the disappearance of Katie Beers. The intersection was a mile from the Spaceplex Family Fun Center—as the crow flies—and search teams had scoured it several times before.

But the police had their reasons: New York Telephone Company computers had tracked down the telephone used to call Linda Inghilleri the day Katie disappeared. It was one of two outdoor pay phones next to a hedge at the large, well-lit, twenty-four-hour Amoco filling station on the northwest corner of Route 347 and Southern Boulevard. Searching the area again made perfect sense—especially after the failure at Esposito's house the day before.

Although they had not told the press, police had known about the phones since the day after the little girl vanished. The phone company had provided printouts of every call made from a pay phone in the vicinity of the amusement center. Both pay phones—and the coins inside them—had been removed and sent to an FBI lab to check for fingerprints. A portable police headquarters unit—essentially an enormous mobile home rigged as an office—had set up shop in the filling station parking lot. And for two days, teams of police searchers had fanned out through fields, woods, backyards, and parking lots between the filling station and Spaceplex.

Today they were going to try a different direction. Instead of again combing the north side of Route 347—also known as the Smithtown Bypass—they were going to examine the south side. There was no particular reason for heading south, except that they never had. "The investigation, unfortunately, hasn't narrowed any further," Dominick Varrone told reporters. "If anything, it's expanded."

Police were moving on other fronts as well. Detectives began looking at parolees in the area who had a history of child abuse. Other cops continued to knock on every door near every home that Katie had ever lived in. They went to her three schools and interviewed her teachers and friends. And they scoured Esposito's neighborhood as well. "We're covering all bases," Detective Varrone frequently told the media. "It's frustrating at times, but we're still optimistic that we're going to discover what happened that day."

The switch in venue, from John Esposito's house in Bay Shore to a filling station in Nesconset several miles away, did not mean the police were giving up on their number one suspect. Quite the contrary.

Although it wasn't widely known at the time, investigators had already determined that the message on Linda Inghilleri's answering machine had been prerecorded. That was one of the reasons they were so interested in the tape recorder instruction manual found in Esposito's house during the search the day before. Where was the tape recorder? What had he done with it?

Another fact grated on detectives. Phone company records showed that whoever called Linda Inghilleri had spent more than half an hour at the Amoco station trying to get through. Her line had been busy all afternoon. The caller had dialed Linda's number eighteen times before finally getting it to ring at 5:06 P.M.

It seemed obvious to Varrone and his underlings that a little girl trying to escape a man with a knife did not have the luxury of placing eighteen phone calls from a pay phone. Besides, the call had been made at a busy service station. Obviously there were other ways for her to have gotten help—if she had been there at all.

Detectives reasoned that a little girl, spending that much time trying to reach two pay phones mounted well above her head, would have been noticed, even in a busy filling station. Surely someone would have spotted a little girl standing hatless and coatless on a damp December evening. But none of the service station employees remembered seeing anything. And the man selling Christmas trees across the street shook his head as police asked questions; he'd been on the corner of that very intersection all afternoon, until late at night. He hadn't seen a thing.

That led Varrone and Company to speculate that someone in a car or a truck had pulled up alongside the two pay phones, kept dialing until Linda Inghilleri got off the line, played a brief tape-recorded message into the phone, and then hung up. And that, as it always seemed to do, brought the task force back to one person: John Esposito.

* * *

In October 1990, Esposito finally found himself a new "little brother." It happened almost by accident.

One Sunday Marilyn Beers and Teddy Rodriguez stopped by Kris Cosme's house in Central Islip. With them were Little John and one of his friends. At the time, Marilyn was baby-sitting for Kris during the week.

In typical adolescent fashion, Little John and his friend wanted away from the adults as fast as possible, before they even got through the front door.

"Where are the nearest stores?" Little John asked.

As Kris gave him directions, her son Anthony, then seven, asked if he could go too. Kris decided to let him tag along, to show them the way.

"Take the back streets, not the main road," she warned. "Go up Cinnamon Street. And don't stay too long."

The boys were gone about half an hour while Marilyn, Teddy, and Kris had coffee at the kitchen table. As soon as the youngsters walked in the door, Little John began a subtle manipulation.

"I'm going to have John pick me up here," he told Marilyn.

"John?" Kris asked.

"He's a friend of mine that Little John goes with every Sunday," Marilyn explained. "He takes him out. Shows him a good time that I can't."

Naturally, Little John had already told Anthony all about his outings with John.

"Oh, Mommy, please, can I go?" Anthony begged Kris.

Kris turned to Marilyn, who assured her John could be trusted. "They go out and do things," Marilyn said. "He takes him to lunch, to the movies."

What could it harm him? thought Kris. It'll give him the day out. Marilyn knows him. It seems like an okay situation.

Anthony joined Little John and Big John on an outing that day in October. They went bowling and roller-skating, and spent a few hours at John's house.

When Anthony Frey got home, he was understandably excited. "Mommy, you have to see it," he told his mother. "He has a whole game room!"

Well, if I want to stop this, I can't, Kris Cosme reasoned to herself. No way. Anthony is totally ecstatic.

She decided to check out Esposito further. So one night she got a baby-sitter and the two of them went out for dinner. Afterwards they went to the movies—and Esposito held her hand. But there was no spark and Kris let it go. She had, after all, just gone through a marital breakup. It was probably too soon for her to see men seriously, she reasoned. She blamed the lack of chemistry on herself.

At the end of that month, John Esposito was hit by the first of two major tragedies that befell him in a matter of months. His younger brother Patrick overdosed on cocaine while driving on the busy Smithtown Bypass. Before losing consciousness, he managed to get the car to the side of the road without causing an accident. He was taken to Stony Brook Hospital and placed on a life-support system. But it was too late, the doctors told the family. He would never recover. The family had Patrick removed from the artificial lung and kidney machines and he died.

Patrick, then just thirty-six, had taken over their father's carpet business on Saxon Avenue just a mile or so south of the Esposito family home, and made a success of it. Too much of a success. The cocaine was just one excess. He had been living in the fast lane, buying a speedboat and a summer house in Kismet on Fire Island.

John was shaken to the core. "Why did he

die?" he kept wailing at Patrick's wake. "Why did he die?"

Rose was also hit hard by her youngest son's death. Her health quickly deteriorated. One night about seven months later, with John at her side, she stopped breathing. He tried mouth-to-mouth resuscitation but it didn't work. Rose was rushed to the hospital. When a doctor told John his mother was unlikely to survive, he fainted. At her funeral, all he did was cry.

The two back-to-back deaths left John depressed and lonely. He told his brother Ron on more than one occasion, "I wish I were dead."

Esposito continued to see Little John and Anthony almost every Sunday. He took them to barbecues and birthday parties at Ron and Joyce's house in nearby Selden. Sometimes, he picked them up on Saturday and the boys spent the night.

Now and then the boys asked to bring friends along on their outings, so Big John developed a system: one week Little John could invite a friend, the next week Anthony could. Every third Sunday it would be just the two boys. Whoever's week it was got to sit in the front seat next to Big John. For the children, that was the most fun of all.

Occasionally, Big John invited along Anthony's sister, Syndel, or Little John's sister, Katie. The girls even stayed over at Esposito's house on Saturday nights along with their brothers.

In the summer of 1991 Big John took Little John, Anthony, his sister-in-law Joan, and Joan's niece Stephanie, age ten, to Orlando, Florida. It was not an inexpensive vacation. They visited Disney World, Sea World, Epcot Center, and Universal Studios and stayed in a hotel inside Disney World for five days. The kids had a great time. Anthony called home every night. On the trip he boasted that he and Stephanie had become boyfriend and girlfriend.

It all seemed like good clean innocent fun. Marilyn Beers and Kris Cosme were pleased. But sometimes there was cause for concern. In the fall of 1991, Anthony came home one Sunday night with a hundred dollars tucked away in his pocket. When his mother questioned him about the money, he told her that Little John had broken into Big John's strongbox with a knife.

"Don't tell anybody we did this," Little John had warned Anthony.

It may have been what Anthony described. Whatever was going on, though, a change had occurred in Big John's relationship with Little

John. One day while they were riding in Esposito's pickup truck, Big John looked over at the youth. John Beers was a budding headbanger with a love for the rock group Kiss. He had long dark hair and tended to black pants, black T-shirts, black leather jackets. He forever had music blaring on the radio or his headset, day and night. And he had taken on the nickname "Maniac." He had become, in short, a full-blown teenager. He was fourteen.

Esposito announced that the friendship was nearing an end.

"You're getting too old," Big John told him. "I'm looking for another boy."

In December 1991—about the time Katie was telling Little John of Sal's abuse—Marilyn Beers called Big Brothers/Big Sisters of Suffolk to check out Esposito. Her son had just dropped a bombshell: he told his mother that Big John had been molesting him for years and had pictures of young boys, naked. Little John said he had seen a videotape in Big John's house. It was titled *Freddie X-rated.*

Executive Director Paul Freedman was in his office early that morning. He picked up the phone.

Marilyn told Freedman about Esposito, saying Big John had been involved with her teenaged son for seven years. He'd spent a lot of time and a lot of money on the boy, who often spent the night at his house. Since Esposito referred to himself as a big brother, she said, a friend had suggested that she check to make sure he was affiliated with the group. She didn't tell Freedman any details of what Little John had told her.

"Let me get back to you," Freedman told her. He hung up and went to his files. Within half an hour he called her back. They talked for about twenty minutes.

"Did your son ever talk about any inappropriate behavior?"

Marilyn wasn't about to tell a stranger over the telephone the things her son had told her. She simply answered no.

Freedman wasn't convinced. He thumbed through Esposito's file, noting his age—early forties—the fact that he had never married, the contrived letter he had sent, and his advertisements for a boy. Now Marilyn was telling him of large gifts and overnight stays. Freedman thought he was seeing a child molester in action.

But he was reluctant to make a definitive statement about Esposito without more information from Little John, something that seemed unlikely at this point. He didn't want to traumatize Marilyn with allegations that might not be true, although he suspected they were. He gave her an answer with kid gloves on.

"It's my advice you tell John Esposito that you don't want him to have anything to do with your son or your family anymore," he told Marilyn. "I think what we're seeing here is the profile of a pedophile."

When they hung up, Freedman called Third Precinct detectives in Bay Shore. An investigator was assigned to check it out. He interviewed both Marilyn and Little John. An embarrassed Little John denied any sex abuse, something he freely admits today.

"Disclosure by a child is rare, especially by an adolescent when confronted with the question," Freedman says. "Often times, with pedophiles, there are dynamics of power and control that are used in the relationship. The children don't see themselves as victims; they interpret it as possibly a homosexual experience or their fault. That's a misinterpretation."

Denial or not, Marilyn was extremely upset. The next day she called Kris. The two women hadn't spoken for months.

It was a Saturday evening, around nine-thirty. Kris's husband-to-be, Juan Cosme, answered the phone and immediately handed it over to Kris. Linda Inghilleri and Marilyn

Beers were on two extensions, both screaming at the same time.

"Do you know John's a pedophilist [*sic*]? Do you know he fits the description of a pedophile? Do you know John's been taking pictures of the kids naked?" they kept shouting.

"Wait a minute, slow down," Kris said.

"Aren't you scared? Aren't you worried? We're never letting Little John go with him again," they chimed.

Kris wasn't convinced. She certainly wasn't going to reject John Esposito on the say-so of these two.

The next day was Sunday, and John was expected to pick up Anthony. Kris left early and took the kids to St. Thomas of Canterbury, an Episcopal church in Smithtown.

Before she left she told Juan, "If John comes, tell him Anthony can't go, and we'll talk when I'm ready to talk."

She let a few weeks pass. Then just before Christmas, John called.

"I'd like to know if I can still give Anthony the Christmas presents I got him," he said.

"Why don't you come over," Kris said. "We need to talk."

They sat down over coffee and talked for more than an hour. Kris told him what Linda and Marilyn had said.

"Yeah, I know," John said. "They were on the phone screaming at me, too. It's because I'm different. They try to label me. It's because I don't have a girlfriend."

"Do you prefer men?" Kris asked.

"No, I prefer to be alone," John said. "I'm a loner. I like to be alone, but I like to help children in any way I can."

He added, "Linda's a troublemaker. She's just making all this up."

What he said rang true. Kris recalled a year earlier when Linda, who had never met Kris, had called Child Protective Services, charging that Kris was unfit to raise children.

"Linda has a way of brainwashing people," Kris told Esposito. "She has a way of making people believe whatever she wants them to believe." With that, she decided to let her son continue to see Esposito. "I'm not going to deny my son the one pleasure I really can't give him," she told Big John.

One Sunday in late February he showed up at Kris's house to pick up Anthony. It was easy for Kris to see that Esposito was upset about something. He was distant, with a troubled look on his face.

"Is Anthony ready?" he asked, seemingly rushed.

"What's wrong, John?" Kris asked.

"I have to go back to the house."

"Why?"

"Little John just suddenly showed up at my doorstep."

"John, tell him to go home," said Kris.

"How can I?"

"John, there's going to be trouble. Knowing Linda, there's going to be trouble."

"I can't disappoint the boy like that. I've had this boy for years."

"Call Marilyn."

"I don't want to get the boy in trouble."

So Big John didn't call Marilyn Beers, and Little John's visits continued. The teen told his mother that he was visiting friends, but then he would take a train from Mastic to Bay Shore to see John.

Finally, in June, Kris convinced Esposito that the deception couldn't continue. She got him to let her call Marilyn while he listened in on an extension.

"Marilyn, I have something to tell you," Kris began.

"Who's this?"

"It's Kris. Marilyn, do you know what your son is doing? Little John is taking it upon himself, behind your back, to show up at Big John's house."

"Oh, yeah," Marilyn said, sighing. "I know. But what am I going to do about it?"

"Marilyn, what happened to that big discussion that we had?"

"What am I going to do? The boy is old enough to have a mind of his own. This is what he wants to do. What am I going to do about it?"

Kris decided to let it drop. If Marilyn wanted to be an ineffectual mother, that was her problem.

John Esposito had another problem at that point, but Kris didn't mention it to Marilyn. He had told her about it a few weeks earlier when he stopped by to pick up Anthony. He had seemed as troubled then as on the day Little John started dropping over.

"John, what's wrong?"

"Oh, I got to work something out."

"Come on, John. We're two adults. We don't hide things from each other. What's wrong?"

He told her that Linda Inghilleri was begging him to take Katie on outings.

"What should I do?"

"John, don't do it," Kris advised. "I don't know what kind of trouble Linda's trying to cause."

But Big John did do it. He didn't mind taking Katie, who was spending a week or more at a time at the Inghilleris' helping out following Linda's leg amputation. But he felt pressured into taking her more often than he wanted. He didn't like it. It disrupted his schedule with Little John and Anthony.

In addition, Katie was often demanding, wheedling and cajoling until she got what she wanted. Everyone at Big John's wound up dancing to Katie's tune, something that annoyed Big John.

Even so, he took her places. The previous summer he had brought her to his twin brother's house in Selden so she could go swimming in the family's pool. Katie, though, was more interested in the ice cream Joyce was handing out. "Can I have more?" Katie asked more than once. "Can I have more?"

Six months later Esposito still had Katie in tow. When he went to pick up Anthony a month before Christmas, he brought Katie along. It was a Saturday night. Kris was home from work early, about seven-fifteen.

"Mommy, look who's here, it's Katie," Syndel said, delighted.

John helped Kris and Juan string Christmas lights and put up the tree. A few weeks later, on a Saturday night, John took Anthony, Syndel, Little John, and Big John's older brother, Billy, to see the Radio City Music Hall Christmas show, the Rockefeller Center Christmas tree, and out to dinner. Shortly after, on Sunday, December 27, he took Little John, Anthony, and Syndel to see *The Bodyguard*.

And the next day he took Katie out for her birthday.

Did anyone think it strange that John Esposito, a lifelong bachelor, spent so much time with children? Did no one question why he never dated, or had any adult friends at all? Certainly the children did not. To them, Big John was an extra-special grown-up friend. To their parents, he was a godsend. Any nagging doubts about the man were pushed aside in light of all his gifts, the outings, the trips to Disney World. The largess of John Esposito was apparently too much to give up.

Esposito has denied he engaged in sex of any kind with the many boys he spent time with. And with the sole exception of Little John, each of the boys has made the same denial. In fact, the boys, and their parents, defend him vigorously. But Paul Freedman has his doubts. "The possibility exists that a personality like Esposito could have a relationship with a series of children and keep it strictly platonic," he says. Indeed, the police have found no reliable evidence that Esposito ever abused the children.

But Esposito's entire pattern of behavior is indicative of pedophilia, Freedman says. He spent inordinate amounts of time and money on boys before they reached puberty and tried to drop them when they got older. At one point he told Kris Cosme that Big Brother policy *required* him to terminate relationships when the little brother turned sixteen, lest there be questions about anything improper going on.

In fact, Freedman says, there was no such rule. The organization no longer sponsors relationships after a little brother or sister turns eighteen. "But a relationship doesn't have to end there just because we put an arbitrary cap on this organization's involvement. A relationship can continue for the rest of their lives."

Shortly after Katie Beers disappeared, Freedman started receiving calls from the press about Esposito. Most reporters wanted to know about Esposito's association with Big Brothers. Freedman held nothing back. He was concerned that someone like Esposito could ruin the reputation of his organization, when, in fact, the group had screened him out.

Afterwards, Freedman started receiving angry calls from Big John's defenders. One woman said her brother had spent a lot of time with Esposito twenty years ago.

"How could you do that to him?" she demanded. "He was a great role model to my brother."

Perhaps, Freedman thought. But he also wondered whether the woman's brother would eventually recall having been the victim of a kind of statutory rape. Often pedophilia victims—male or female—don't remember the sexual abuse because it is too painful. "It takes years," Freedman says. "Sometimes half a lifetime."

And even then the victim may not want to talk about it. Even Little John Beers keeps it vague. "He [Esposito] sexually molested me in ways I'm not getting into," he has said. "It started when I was seven. I don't remember when it stopped."

In the weeks after his sister's disappearance, Little John changed his story more than once. Even the police do not know whether to believe Little John, and no charges have been filed based on his claims. "He's shot his credibility," says Freedman. But he wasn't surprised. "It's a pattern to be expected," he says. "If there was anything that might move John Beers to a disclosure at all, it was the trauma of Katie Beers."

Chapter Twelve

BY NEW YEAR'S DAY, the fifth day of Katie Beers's disappearance, Linda Inghilleri was getting on everyone's nerves—especially the police and press.

Reporters were particularly frustrated with the erratic way she gave out interviews. On January 1, for example, she and Sal refused to speak to any of the newspaper reporters or photographers gathered outside her house.

Sometime that afternoon, a veteran *Newsday* photographer arrived and knocked at the door.

"We're not giving out any—," Sal began.

"Listen, just give me a cup of coffee, okay?" the photographer said. "I'm off in twenty minutes. Let me make a picture and get my coffee and I'm out of here."

Sal shrugged, said, "Okay," and invited the

photographer in. He got both his picture and a cup of coffee—while outside four rival photographers steamed.

Earlier that same day, Linda had inexplicably given an extensive television interview to Channel 7 and then slammed the door in the face of a reporter from a rival television station who showed up a few minutes later. Two days later, Linda would sit down and speak to the reporter she had refused to see.

"Linda, if you want to help find Katie you should talk to everybody," the reporter admonished.

"I thought all you guys shared film," Linda replied.

The reporter tried to keep from laughing. "Nope," she said, straight-faced. "We don't share."

On another day, Linda gave an hour-long interview to *New York Post* reporter Kieran Crowley. Then she screamed, "Get the fuck out of my house," to a magazine reporter who had been waiting patiently in the living room at the invitation of Sal.

Outside, the magazine reporter was puzzled.

"What's the deal?" she asked Crowley. "How come you got in and I didn't?"

"It is your misfortune to have been born a beautiful young woman and not a handsome young man," Crowley joked. "Sorry."

* * *

Linda also annoyed the police when she decided to turn to psychics. As a rule, police departments do not have a total knee-jerk reaction against psychics. They will take any help they can get. On the other hand, most detectives believe psychics are an incredible waste of time. With some notable exceptions, the information they provide in missing person cases is usually not that helpful. And sometimes psychics get underfoot.

As far as detectives were concerned, that proved to be the case with the first psychic who tried to find Katie, John Monti of Eastport, Long Island. But for Marilyn, at least, he proved to be a good friend.

Getting him wasn't easy. When Linda decided she wanted psychic help, she began by telephoning a John Monti that she found in the Suffolk telephone directory. It wasn't the right John Monti but he was kind enough to relay her call to the psychic. Even so, Monti never even spoke with Linda. Every time he visited her house, she was so busy with the press that he was forced to talk to Sal.

"I want to talk to John Esposito," Monti declared.

Sal brightened. "We have the same lawyers, the Sibens," he replied. "Talk to them."

Andrew Siben was not thrilled with Monti's call.

"I want to talk to John Esposito," Monti demanded. "We have a party here that's guilty of holding the girl. I would like to talk to him. Maybe it could come to some kind of conclusion."

Siben ended the conversation right there. "I don't think that would be in the best interests of my client," he said. "Thank you very much." And he hung up the phone.

Monti was undeterred. He again tried to talk to Linda but she continued to be too busy. So he drove thirty-five miles east and dropped in on Marilyn in Mastic Beach. Little John answered the door and invited him in.

"My mother has been looking for you," Little John told him. "We've heard about you."

Monti and Marilyn sat down at the table in the Beers' cluttered kitchen. She gave Monti some pictures of Katie but seemed matter-of-fact, almost cold, about her daughter's future.

"If John has Katie, I hope he takes care of her," she told Monti. "And if Linda has her, I hope she does, too. They always did in the past."

On New Year's Day Monti showed up at the intersection of Route 347 and Southern Boulevard in Nesconset where police were conducting a full-scale search. He walked into a wooded area where he told reporters he could "feel" Katie had been chased. Angry police told him to leave, that he was interfering with their investigation.

Monti also told reporters that day that Katie was alive and would stay alive through New Year's weekend. When Linda saw a televised report of his predictions that evening, she gained renewed hope. "I believe in psychics," she said. "It doesn't surprise me what he said. I believe what he is saying is true."

The next day, January 2, another psychic, Helen Legotti, from Lindenhurst, visited Linda and Marilyn at Linda's house in Bay Shore. Linda had contacted her by dialing 1-800-HELP-A-KID, a national organization that helps trace missing children.

When Legotti arrived, the Inghilleri kitchen was packed with people. Ann Butler was cooking pork chops, police were manning the phones, and Linda and Marilyn were sitting at the round kitchen table.

Surprisingly, Linda was shaking with fear.

"I'm terrified of you," she said.

"I'm not here to harm you, I'm here to help you," Legotti replied.

"I hope you're not going to say personal

things about me at the table," Linda said, motioning to all the people in the room.

Linda had been calling 900-number psychics ever since Katie disappeared, asking if Katie was alive. Legotti, who has white hair and intense looks, believes that she frightened Linda because she looks—and acts—different from most psychics. "I'm a professional," she says.

Within minutes of Legotti's arrival, Marilyn left the room.

"Where's Marilyn?" Legotti asked.

"Oh, she went inside," Linda answered.

Legotti followed Marilyn into the living room. "I'd like you here," she said.

"Oh, I didn't know that," Marilyn said.

"You *are* Katie's mother. I'd like to speak with you."

For the next three hours, Legotti asked Linda and Marilyn about various clues she was picking up. Every time she asked a question, Linda answered. "Linda's a very controlling, intimidating person," Legotti decided. "She controls Marilyn."

So Legotti tried to ask Marilyn questions directly. Each time, Linda interrupted. Finally, Legotti had had enough. "I'd like to speak to Marilyn," she told Linda. "I'd like to hear what she says."

Linda quieted down for a while as Marilyn answered some of the psychic's questions. But it soon became clear that Linda didn't like what she was hearing. At one point, Legotti asked about Esposito and Marilyn got angry.

"There was an order of protection against Esposito," Marilyn snapped, throwing a glance Linda's way. "He wasn't supposed to be around Katie."

"I just found out about that," Linda cut in defensively. "I never knew that. Nobody told me."

Marilyn would have none of it. "I *told* you, 'Do not have him in this house when my daughter is here,' " she replied angrily.

Throughout the session Linda repeatedly wanted to know about Katie. "Is Katie alive?" she asked.

Legotti wouldn't answer. She explained that she had been looking for missing children for thirteen years and she couldn't say.

"I don't advise dead or alive," she said. "Just get her back. No matter what condition. I deal with people that have their children gone and never will find them and they're in limbo the rest of their lives."

Actually, Legotti did have an idea that Katie was alive, but she didn't want to tell the women under what circumstances. She kept seeing

Katie underground. "I thought, My God, I don't believe she's dead. I kept feeling Esposito didn't kill her, and yet I saw Katie buried," she later recalled. "If I had just gotten into Esposito's house, I would have known."

She asked if she could meet Esposito but neither Linda nor Marilyn thought that could be arranged. But Linda suggested it might be possible to talk to him on the phone. She called from the kitchen phone while Legotti listened in on an extension in the bedroom.

"I need to tune in to his voice," Legotti explained before they called. "You need to ask him about some of the psychic feelings I'm having. There's something about Lake Ronkonkoma. Does he have property there? There's something about that."

At first Esposito didn't want to talk. Police won't say, but there seems little doubt that his phone was being tapped by the kidnapping task force. Esposito began whispering, as if his listeners wouldn't be able to hear him if he spoke softly. "I can't talk to you," he said. "I'm not supposed to be on the phone."

"Please, John, I need to talk to you," Linda begged.

For the next twenty minutes Legotti listened as Linda kept Esposito on the line.

"Did you ever take Katie to Lake Ronkonkoma?" she asked.

John said that he hadn't. Then he began to cry. "I'm not supposed to be talking to you," he said.

"Please, John, don't hang up," Linda pleaded. "I just want to speak to you. I want to talk about Katie. I miss her so much."

Crying, Esposito hung up.

On Sunday, January 3, Linda planned to bring in another psychic, a channeler who was going to try to contact Katie spiritually. That morning, Linda told Marilyn to take the train back to Mastic to get Little John. Linda wanted the teen present so the psychic could get better vibes about Katie.

A reporter, hanging out at the house in Bay Shore, offered to give Marilyn a ride. They drove the thirty-five miles to Mastic and the reporter dropped her off. Marilyn then went inside the garage apartment and tried to get Little John to return with her to Bay Shore.

He refused.

Within minutes they were arguing. Then shouting. Then screaming. Marilyn pulled Little John's hair. He hit her several times.

The Beerses' landlord, Ralph Salzillo, who lived in the main house, overheard the ruckus and called the police at 12:45 P.M. When a cop car arrived at 1:10 P.M., patrolmen found the two on the kitchen floor. Marilyn was holding Little John in a headlock.

Marilyn had several cuts on the left side of her forehead. She was treated and released at Brookhaven Memorial Hospital in Patchogue.

Little John was charged with third-degree assault and held until his father, Teddy Rodriguez, posted twenty-five dollars bail at 4:45 P.M. They left the police station without talking to reporters.

Rodriguez, a landscaper who had been on disability since injuring his back three years before, says Suffolk County police had never questioned him—or even knew he existed—until he got Little John out of jail that Saturday. Detectives asked him a few questions, he says, but never considered him a serious suspect in the case. He and Marilyn had seen each other off and on over the years but he remained married to his wife, Nilza.

At one point, though, Rodriguez *was* the focus of police interest. A correspondent for one of New York's television stations noticed that he had a small tattoo on his hand that looked like a cross and wondered if it was the sign of Santería, a religious sect that slaughters animals in sacrifice to the saints. Perhaps Katie's disappearance had to do with a cult, she thought.

The day the TV reporter planned to ask about it, the running feud between Marilyn Beers and Linda Inghilleri reached new heights of angry passion. Sal Inghilleri announced that Marilyn was into witchcraft and voodoo.

Oh, shit, you're blowing my story, the TV reporter thought.

Later, at her own press conference, Marilyn denied the witchcraft charge. She said her experience in the occult went no deeper than having a few books on the subject.

"I know Linda's saying I'm a witch and Teddy's a warlock," she told reporters.

"Are you?" asked Kieran Crowley of the *New York Post*.

"Don't be ridiculous," she replied. "All I have is a Ouija board."

Later, a detective privately told the TV reporter that the police had, in fact, investigated Teddy's tattoo and determined it wasn't cultlike.

"Even if it was Santería, even if it was true, they don't do human sacrifices," the cop reassured the reporter.

Linda and Marilyn were not the only people using psychics to find Katie Beers. On the morning of Monday, January 4, the one-week anniversary of little Katie's disappearance, private detective Richie Haeg was in his office in Coram when he got a frantic visitor: his letter carrier, Janet Russell.

She told Haeg's office manager, Linda Buttacavoli, that she had been having visions about Katie Beers for days. She *had* to talk to Haeg immediately. Haeg, who had worked on Amy Fisher's defense before she was sent to prison, always had time for odd cases.

Janet's visions were laden with detail. "I see her in a lean-to, with three sides, no front, the kind of place you store a dog or wood in," she told the investigator. "She's chained around the neck, but she isn't crying anymore. She's sick. She's having respiratory problems."

"Where is this?" Haeg asked.

"I see a green house with white shutters. It's dark. It's in Central Islip. There's something about a lady with red hair. She's wearing a wig. The kid is there. I can feel it."

Haeg pulled out a map of Suffolk County and Janet pointed out where she believed Katie Beers was located. It was near the Bayard Cutting Arboretum in Central Islip.

The investigator mulled over what he had just heard. This is crazy, he thought. But—God forbid—there's a one-in-a-million chance that

Janet-from-another-planet has some kind of ability. We better check this out.

He called a high-ranking detective he knew on the kidnapping task force and told him what Janet had envisioned. The detective didn't laugh but didn't offer to send any help either.

So Haeg drafted one of his investigators and the two drove to Central Islip looking for a lean-to at a green house with white shutters. They walked around in the cold for nearly three hours. Haeg was right; it *was* a million-to-one shot. He didn't find it.

A few days later, yet another psychic, Linda Panciarello, forty-eight, entered the picture. This time there was progress of sorts.

On the evening of January 7, Panciarello stood in Katie's bedroom in Linda Inghilleri's home. At about 7:30 P.M, she held Katie's black velour headband for a few minutes and then asked Sal to join her in the room. She said she needed more of Katie's energy.

She opened a desk drawer, pulled out an *Aladdin* coloring book, and began flipping through the pages. Suddenly a letter dropped out and onto the floor. It was written on a cream-colored piece of construction paper folded like a card. On the front, the words "I love you" were written with a green felt-tip pen.

When opened up, the left half featured a heart with "I love you" six more times, this time with a black felt marker.

On the right side was a letter written in a child's hand, with plenty of misspellings and grammatical errors:

Dear Aunt Linda:

I love you. You are my favorite person in the world but I am stuck in the middle . . . it is very hard for me to decide who I want to live with Because I have lived with yo both.

Love always,

Katherine.

P.S. I love you.

Linda Inghilleri saw the note as a positive sign, a hint that Katie had run away because of the tensions between her two mothers. Marilyn Beers, however, labeled the note a fake, pointing out that misspellings were uncharacteristic of Katie. As further proof, she said that Katie always called her "Mom," a point that became a major subject of dispute in the Inghilleri-Beers Wars for many weeks.

In any event, Linda Inghilleri turned the letter over to the police that very evening. No one from the kidnapping task force would talk about the note for the record, but it was clear that detectives were not impressed. "After ten days, all of a sudden this comes up," an exasperated law enforcement official told *Newsday*. "I think the whole situation is a series of bizarre incidents that don't add up. Every day something new pops up. We don't know what this is."

The letter also provoked some sniping from other psychics. Helen Legotti charged that the note had been planted by Linda Inghilleri for Panciarello to find. "The woman fell for it," she insisted. "It was a setup. I feel strongly that Linda put the letter in there, and that woman walked right into it."

In the basement of the Fourth Precinct in Hauppauge, where the kidnapping task force had set up headquarters, nerves were getting frayed. The police had interviewed hundreds of people as they followed countless leads. They felt tantalizingly close to breaking the case. But nothing was happening. Every clue they had led to one man, someone they thought would crack under pressure. But he had not cracked.

The detectives started taking it out on each

other. Tempers flared. There were more than a few arguments.

"You've got a lot of cops who want to solve a puzzle and they get involved," said one task force insider. "About the third day, they're getting by on about four hours' sleep. They go to work; they get home at midnight, one in the morning. Their entire personal life is turned upside down. These are good cops; they're good problem solvers. They're working two, three, four days and there's no light at the end of the tunnel. Frustration sets in. Even to the point of tempers. It's human nature. It's justified."

Varrone struggled to keep personality conflicts to a minimum. In daily skull sessions he and his staff traded theories and possibilities. Always, Varrone encouraged his staff to think optimistically.

But sometimes driving home late at night, after a long day with little progress, Varrone found himself discouraged. He knew John Esposito had something to do with Katie's disappearance. He was simply afraid that his task force was too late.

When he all but lost hope that little Katie Beers might still be alive somewhere, Dominick Varrone turned to his family for inspiration. It was always there. All he had to do was gaze at his ten-year-old daughter, Katherine, to remember why a little girl with short dark blond hair and a sunny smile meant so much. It made him all the more resolved to find her.

Chapter Thirteen

KATIE BEERS lay in her cell and closed her eyes. In *Beauty and the Beast*, she knew, the townsfolk came to rescue Beauty when she was being held prisoner in the Beast's castle. In another of her favorite Disney films, *One Hundred and One Dalmatians*, the puppies were saved from the evil Cruella de Vil by their parents Pongo and Perdita. And in *Aladdin*, which she had seen twice, the hero was liberated from the Cave of Wonders by a magic carpet and a genie. But there had been no townspeople, no Pongo and Perdita, no magic carpet or genie here.

She thought of *The Wizard of Oz*, not the movie but the book her mother had given her for Christmas. She had never been a reader but this book had caught her fancy; she had read all 215 pages before leaving to visit Aunt Linda.

At least Dorothy had found new friends on the other side of the rainbow; Katie had no one. There were no lions, tin woodmen, or straw men to help her. She scrunched her face up tight and made a wish. "There's no place like home," she whispered over and over. "There's no place like home." But when she opened her eyes, she was still there.

Every day the cops put a little more pressure on John Esposito. They continued to follow him everywhere, staying so close that he felt like the president of the United States with a phalanx of Secret Service agents close behind. But now that their search had failed to find anything, they dreamed up reasons to stop by and talk to him. Or to stop by and talk to his family or his lawyers.

Their latest gambit was to try to talk Esposito into taking a lie detector test. It couldn't be used as evidence against him, they reasoned; no court would permit it. And if he passed, the cops would leave him alone. Detectives talked to Esposito about it directly and to his twin brother Ron.

On January 8, two detectives stopped by Esposito's house to clarify some point about Katie's pocketbook. They were less interested in the answers they received than they were in letting Esposito know that he wasn't off the hook.

It may have been a fortuitous coincidence that police were present at the very moment the evening news came on that night. Or it may have been a deliberate ploy on the part of the police. In any event, the TV was on in the background, tuned to WABC-TV's *Eyewitness News*. Esposito and the detectives paused automatically when correspondent N. J. Burkett came on with a report on the Katie Beers case. Suffolk County investigators were now saying that Katie's screaming telephone call the night she vanished was a tape recording. FBI tests had shown that she had not spoken directly into the telephone.

Esposito was clearly unnerved. "You could almost see the air go out of his balloon," a police officer said. "He was visibly shaken. Now he knew that everyone else knew."

The detectives continued to talk to Esposito but didn't push him too hard. Actually, if they had to swear to it, they liked Big John. He seemed like a nice guy. Still, each of them knew he had something to do with Katie's disappearance. No question about it.

"You keep talking to him," the cop later explained. "You hope for that spark of morality, give him an avenue to tell you what really happened. He locked into his story and didn't dance from it too much. Proving a hunch is very difficult. He was the last one to see her, so that makes him the first one we look at."

Esposito may have been upset about what he saw on the evening news. But he may also have been relieved that the police had come and gone. That meant he could visit Katie in relative safety.

He was always reluctant to bring her food and let her go to the bathroom. What if the cops showed up when he was down there? They would discover everything.

But tonight would be good. The odds were good that the cops wouldn't come back a second time. He checked his watch; he had plenty of time. He put some food together in a plastic grocery bag and stepped into the small office off his kitchen. He reached up to a stereo speaker and pushed a button embedded in the cloth front. It masked an infant monitor, the one-way walkie-talkie that parents put in a child's nursery so that they can hear if there is trouble.

"I'm coming down, Katie," he said.

He then removed two baseball caps hanging from white hooks just under the top of the stereo cabinet that had been custom-built into a wall in his office. Behind each hook was a bolt, which he unscrewed. When he pulled them out, they were each three inches long. His next move was to bend over and take out the lowest shelf of the cabinet. It was covering two more three-inch bolts. He unscrewed those as well. After that, he slid a set of casters under the front of the cabinet and rolled the stereo unit out of the wall; the rear already had its own set of wheels.

To the right of the cabinet was a closet. He opened the door and went inside. Where the stereo cabinet had been was now vacant. He rolled back the brown carpet and the foam matting on the floor and lifted up a layer of linoleum, revealing a concrete slab. Embedded in the slab was a steel eyebolt. Above it, hidden behind a shelf support in the closet, was a chain, which he now fastened to the eyebolt. The chain was threaded through a block and tackle and connected to some weights. Esposito used the weights to help lift the concrete, a two-hundred-pound slab.

Beneath the slab was a plywood trapdoor. He raised it and lowered himself into a seven-foot vertical shaft. Two-by-fours at regular intervals acted as slats in a ladder so that he could easily climb down. At the bottom was a five-foot-long tunnel leading to a sealed plywood hatch. He used an electric tool to undo several screws that were holding the hatch in place. After pulling away the plywood, he squeezed through, bringing the bag of food with him. Katie was there waiting for him.

He checked his watch. It was well before 8:00 P.M. Good. There was a television program that evening that he wanted to watch with Katie. The Fox channel in New York City was showing *America's Most Wanted.* He had read about it in the paper that day. Katie was going to be the featured missing child.

Linda Inghilleri sat in her kitchen, tears streaking her cheeks as she listened to the boom box on her table. She was playing the theme song of the movie, *Aladdin*. It was Katie's favorite song and Linda had been playing it all day. As soon as the music ended, she rewound the tape and turned it on again, just as she had with Katie's frantic message on her answering machine the night the little girl disappeared.

"Listen to the words," Linda told a visitor. "Listen."

She cried some more. The song was about romance and travel; in the film, Aladdin takes Princess Jasmine to exciting places around the world. Maybe Katie got the same idea.

Now Linda was hoping that the same lyrics could bring her back. She was going to try to get a local radio station to play the song—with a dedication to Katie from her family. That way Katie would know that she had left behind people who were thinking of her.

"If she hears this song, she will know our feelings," Linda said. "This song tells her there's a place she can go where there's happiness, love, and peace."

A few days later, on January 12, private investigator Richie Haeg was on a stakeout in Mastic Beach when his cellular phone rang. It was Eric Naiburg, a well-known Long Island attorney.

Haeg and Naiburg had known each other for years. Until recently they had worked together on the Amy Fisher case. Haeg had investigated the affair between Amy and Joey Buttafuoco, interviewing friends of Amy's, as well as co-workers of Joey's who claimed to have seen the pair together.

This time, Naiburg wanted to talk about Katie Beers. "Should we try to raise some money for this kid?" he asked Haeg. "Why don't you go talk to the mother? Tell her I can help her."

"No problem," Haeg said. "I'm in Mastic

Beach anyway. Actually, I think I'm around the corner."

A few minutes later, Haeg dropped in to see Marilyn. Lingering outside the house were two Suffolk County detectives, Dennis Rafferty and Ray Kelly. Haeg had worked with both of them over the years when he was a Suffolk County detective himself. They chatted briefly. Then Haeg went in to speak to Marilyn.

He sat down in her messy living room and talked to her and her mother for about ten minutes. "If you need help raising money, Eric can help you," he told Marilyn. "Eric can also help you with movie deals. He's just done it on the Amy Fisher case."

Marilyn listened, chain-smoking. "Right now, all I'm interested in is getting Katie back," she said.

"This might help," Haeg told her. "Call me if you need anything."

He left her his card.

Haeg stepped outside. For the next twenty minutes he spoke to the detectives. They told him how frustrating the case was, and how many different directions they'd been going in. Before he left, Haeg wished them luck.

That same day, Suffolk County Police Commissioner Peter Cosgrove and District Attorney

James Catterson, Jr., issued the following joint press release:

> It is now 15 days since the sudden unexplained disappearance of Katie Beers. No effort has been spared by the Suffolk County law enforcement community to follow every lead in an attempt to locate her and identify those responsible for her disappearance. Understandably the human drama presented by the plight of this 10-year-old little girl has sparked enormous media interest as witnessed by the daily intense coverage both in newspapers and on radio and television. Unfortunately as day follows day the media's efforts to report further developments have at times hindered police investigators who are primarily responsible for bringing this case to a definitive conclusion. While we are mindful that ofttimes media attention is case-beneficial, nonetheless there are occasions when law enforcement activities may actually be thwarted and/or short-circuited by undue exposure or discussion of circumstances and hitherto unpublished "facts." Accordingly, until further notice, Suffolk County law enforcement officials and personnel will decline to re-

> spond to media inquiries concerning any aspect of this investigation. We request the media's understanding and cooperation in this information embargo.

Usually news blackouts in kidnapping cases are called at the very beginning, to avoid interfering in delicate ransom negotiations. But in this case, it was clear, there had been no ransom demands and there were no negotiations. The only communication with Katie or her abductors, if there were any, had been the message received by Linda Inghilleri the day the girl disappeared.

This news blackout was born out of frustration. From the first day, the press had been ahead of the police, and detectives were not happy. Many of the people they were debriefing had already given extensive interviews to television and print reporters.

"The problem is that after people finish talking to the press, they give the *Reader's Digest* version to the cops," one officer groused. "We'd rather have the first response."

As it happened, there was plenty of news to report that day without police cooperation. Katie had been spotted. Two people in Dutchess County, due north of New York City, said they had seen her at a Grand Union supermarket in

Hyde Park, New York. One of the witnesses, a sixteen-year-old girl, said she saw a little girl resembling Katie get out of a brown station wagon with no coat on and rush to a pay phone. Two men jumped out of the car after her. One of the men slapped her hand away from the phone and they led her back to the car.

A few days later police staked out the supermarket, hoping to see the girl again. The child didn't show up, but police did find a store employee who remembered seeing the little girl spending an inordinate amount of time in one of the aisles. Later, the same employee spotted the brown station wagon idling in an out-of-the-way spot near the store.

Was this the break the police had been waiting for? Detectives knew not to get their hopes up. The day before, a Spanish-speaking Bay Shore mechanic had come forward, saying he had given Katie Beers a ride that morning. And more than fifty people had telephoned police with tips after seeing Katie's story on *America's Most Wanted.* All of the tips had been gratefully checked out. But none of them had led to anything.

That night John Esposito went down to see Katie. It was a somber occasion. Esposito knew that this was going to be his last trip to the dungeon. Before he could tell Katie what he had come to say, she told him that she didn't feel well. She said she needed to see a doctor and begged him to let her go.

He turned her down. "You're going to have to wait," he told her. He was going to hang himself that night, he explained. He would pin a note on his body somewhere describing where she was. The police would find her in a day. She could go to the doctor then.

Katie started to cry. "I want to go home. Please, John, let me go home," she pleaded.

He simply shook his head and cried. Then he handed her five hundred dollars in cash. Police believed it was to ensure her silence: a bribe for her not to talk about what had happened in the dungeon.

And then he left. That night Katie Beers was more afraid than she had ever been in her entire life. What if he hanged himself and didn't leave a note? No one would ever find her. What if he just left her there to starve to death? Why would he give her money if he planned to die? None of it made any sense. She would not sleep at all that night.

After Esposito returned the stereo cabinet to its home in the wall, tightened the bolts, and rehung his baseball caps, he picked up the telephone and called Anthony Frey.

It was about 8:30 P.M. Kris Cosme answered the phone. She told Esposito that the family had not opened the gingerbread house that he had gotten them for Christmas.

"John, we decided we're not going to open this gingerbread house until you're out of trouble," she said.

Then she handed the phone to Anthony. They talked for about fifteen minutes.

"I'm sorry for everything that's going on," John told the child. "I know you're upset. Please don't be upset. Don't hate me for this. I'm sorry for everything. Don't worry about anything. I know Katie will be found. I know she will."

"I know you can't pick us up," Anthony said, "but I really miss you."

"I miss you, too," John said. "I miss you, too."

Chapter Fourteen

IT DIDN'T SEEM like that big a deal. The day after New Year's, Sidney Siben began a ten-day vacation in Florida and left his partners, including his nephew Andrew, in charge of their law firm. But it was a very big deal to John Esposito. And, although they didn't know it at the time, it was a big deal to Suffolk's kidnapping task force—and an even bigger one for Katie Beers.

Siben had scheduled himself to be out of the office from January 2 through January 12. While he was gone, Esposito called Siben's secretary several times, checking on when the attorney would return. The answer came back every time: "Wednesday."

On Tuesday, January 12, Esposito checked again.

"Mr. Siben will definitely be in tomorrow," she reassured him.

On Wednesday, Esposito got an early start. Sometime before 9:00 A.M. he called his brother Ronnie and sister-in-law Joyce at their home in Selden.

"I am going to see the lawyer and I need you guys," he told them. He asked them to meet him at Siben's office as soon as they could get there. "There's something I have to tell you," he explained.

He also called Joanie, his brother Pat's widow, who lived nearby. He asked her to go with him to Siben's office on Main Street in Bay Shore, about two miles from the Esposito home.

He walked in, unannounced, at about 9:30 A.M. and got in to see his attorney a few minutes later. Siben looked tanned and rested after more than a week in the Florida sun.

The two men sat down in Siben's large, windowed office on the second floor and Esposito got straight to the point.

"I know where Katie is," he said.

The news was too enormous to grasp the first time. "What do you mean?" Siben asked.

"I know where she is," Esposito repeated.

This time Siben understood.

"Is she alive?"

"Yes."

"Where is she?"

"She's in my house."

Siben didn't believe him. "Cut it out, John. There are three cops living there around the clock."

"No, really. I've been bringing her food from the 7-Eleven."

The attorney still didn't know whether to believe his client but he did know that he would have to act. Before continuing, he excused himself for a moment and stepped outside to the waiting room.

Joan Esposito was seated there by herself. Siben told her to contact the rest of the family and have them come to the office as soon as possible.

"If what he's telling me is true, we should tell the D.A.," Siben told her. "If we do, he's going to be arrested."

Joan told Siben that Esposito had already contacted his brother Ron and sister-in-law Joyce. They were on their way from Selden, a lengthy drive.

Siben nodded and went back into his office. This time Esposito told him about the bunker.

"Nobody can get in there but me," he said.

"Why?"

"I have this two-hundred-pound block on this underground chamber I built. If you get in there and you don't know exactly how to remove it, it will fall. Katie will be killed."

Siben still didn't believe his client. But that was irrelevant. He asked his nephew Andrew and another attorney, Ira Kash, to meet with the district attorney at once. Before they left, they, too, questioned Esposito.

Esposito said, "I know where Katie is. I know she's alive. I know where she's being held. I want to see her released."

"Where is she, John?" asked Andrew Siben.

"She's in my house. She's behind the wall. I've had her there the whole time."

They questioned him further, and then asked him to sign a waiver allowing them to go to the police with the information and releasing them from their responsibility to honor the attorney-client privilege. Esposito did so at once.

While the lawyers were traveling to the district attorney's office in Hauppauge, Ronnie and Joyce Esposito arrived at Siben & Siben. Esposito—"Johnny" to his siblings and their spouses—met with them in the lobby.

"She's at the house," he told them. "She's underground."

"What do you mean, Johnny?" asked Joyce, gently. "There is no basement."

"No, you don't understand," Esposito said. "She's behind a wall."

The family stayed together in the attorney's office while they waited. Each knew it might be the last time they could all be together without the authorities standing guard.

Esposito told Siben that he had originally built the dungeon in case of a nuclear attack.

He also said that Katie went willingly into hiding because she wanted to escape her family.

At about 11:00 A.M., a lawyer called a *Newsday* reporter, who shared the news with managing editor Howard Schneider. Schneider is someone who can get overly excited about anything, even dust. An authorized history of the paper, *Newsday: A Candid History of the Respectable Tabloid* by Robert F. Keeler, describes him as "enthusiasm incarnate."

So when confronted with the possibility of real news, he automatically went into overdrive. He called Suffolk editor Miriam Pawel into his office and less than a minute later she was rounding up reporters. She sent two to Esposito's house and others to the Fourth Precinct in Hauppauge, to the Sibens' office, to the district attorney's office, the Beers house in Mastic, and the Inghilleri house in Bay Shore. By 12:30, ten *Newsday* reporters were in place, ready to cover Katie's release.

But nothing was happening.

There was no activity anywhere, especially at John Esposito's house on North Saxon Avenue. Reporters, under orders to phone in every five minutes, said the place was deserted. They saw no one, including cops.

Newsday has a long history of prodding slow-moving local officials into doing their jobs, especially on major stories with looming deadlines. This was no exception.

"Where are the cops?" asked Jim Mulvaney, who was helping run operations at the newspaper. "What would be the justification for them not being there?"

He began to wonder if the leak was true. He paced and thought hard. He was a former police reporter whose father, Jim Senior, was a legendary defense attorney in Queens. Mulvaney knew how the system worked.

Are the cops still negotiating with this guy? he asked himself. Are they waiting to get an ambulance together? Are they waiting for a prosecutor to be on the scene? Are they waiting for the mother to get there? Linda? This doesn't make any sense.

Finally, he turned to his colleagues. "There is no justification," he said. "The only explanation possible is that they don't know."

Miriam Pawel agreed. She asked a reporter to try to reach the kidnapping task force.

"If you're going to tell the cops, I'll tell the D.A.," Mulvaney said. "I can get through. I used to drink in his bar."

When Mulvaney covered cops, he used to hang out at the Printer's Devil, a Port Jefferson bar owned by an up-and-coming prosecutor named James Catterson. Catterson, now the district attorney, and Mulvaney had always had a good working relationship. Also, Mulvaney figured that Catterson saw him as someone from his own generation, not one of the myriad younger faces on the paper's staff.

It'll be easy for me to get through, Mulvaney thought, because he's not mad at me for anything.

Mulvaney also knew not to call directly. He first asked for another person in Catterson's office.

"He's not in," came the answer.

So Mulvaney asked for someone else on the staff, an investigator. "This is about Katie Beers," he explained. "I think I know where she is. Somebody's got to do something."

"He's in with Catterson."

"Let me talk to Catterson."

There was a pause. Mulvaney was switched to Catterson's secretary.

"It's Jim Mulvaney, *Newsday*," he said. "I need to speak to Catterson."

"He isn't in," the secretary said quickly. "He'll be glad to call you back."

"I know he's in there. This is a life-and-death matter about Katie Beers. Tell him who it is."

Moments later, Catterson picked up the phone.

"Jimmy," he said. "How are you?"

"Look, we have been told that the girl is alive and at John Esposito's house, hidden behind a false wall."

Catterson tried not to sound surprised. "Jim, I'm in negotiations now with Esposito's lawyer," he said. There was a pause. Mulvaney heard Catterson say, annoyed, "Tell [Chief of

Detectives Thomas] Blomberg to get to the house."

Mulvaney threw in a quick disclaimer. "I'm not swearing by any of this," he said. "It's secondhand, what I'm telling you. You know we're not trying to be part of the story. We just want to do what's right here."

"I appreciate that," Catterson said. "Thanks very much."

By 1:30 P.M. a crowd had gathered outside Esposito's house, and police erected a roadblock.

As Siben got ready to take his client to the house, he decided to sneak Esposito down the office fire escape. It would be easier, what with all the reporters gathering outside.

Esposito seemed low and miserable. "I think I'm going to kill myself," he told Siben.

With that, Siben guided Esposito toward a back set of stairs and the rear door. He couldn't risk the fire escape, he decided. If he jumps, he thought to himself, the little girl will die.

They went out a back door and got into a white Nissan along with two members of Siben's staff. As they drove up North Saxon Avenue, Siben was still unsure that Esposito was telling the truth.

I still think he's pulling my leg, Siben thought.

On the way they met Andrew Siben in another car and followed him to Esposito's house.

They arrived around 2:00 P.M. The place was a madhouse; television trucks, camera crews, reporters, photographers, neighbors, and cops surrounded the Esposito compound.

They had to park some distance from the house and walk in. Once inside police lines, however, things were much calmer. Around 2:10 they were ready to go. All in all, roughly eight men followed John Esposito into his reconverted garage behind the house: Sidney and Andrew Siben and a crew of detectives.

They crowded into Esposito's small office off the kitchen and watched in wonder as he pushed the front of a stereo speaker with his finger. "Katie," he said. "I'm coming down."

Chapter Fifteen

DOWNSTAIRS, Katie breathed something of a sigh of relief. Big John hadn't killed himself. There was hope for her yet. On the other hand, it wasn't over. Who could tell what would happen next? And so she lay in fear, unaware of what was going on above her.

Upstairs, everyone from Andrew Siben to the detectives watched in wonder as John Esposito removed the two baseball caps from their white hooks and unscrewed the three-inch bolts beneath. When he rolled out the stereo cabinet, the detectives cringed. During their many searches, they hadn't taken the house apart as they might have during a drug raid. If they had, this might have been over a lot sooner.

Still, when Esposito rolled back the carpet and lifted the linoleum, the detectives could see that they might have missed the concrete slab altogether—even if they had torn down the entire house. Esposito had a reputation for being an accomplished builder; what they were seeing that afternoon was proof of that.

After Esposito raised the concrete slab, detectives took over. They were not going to let him into the vertical shaft alone. One of the detectives lowered himself into the hole and squeezed through the five-foot tunnel. Esposito had already shown him how to use the tool to remove the final door.

The detective was gone for what seemed like a very long time.

Upstairs, the mood was tense. John Esposito stood silently, his head bowed. The detectives did not speak either. Their eyes were glued to the open hatch. As the days following Katie's disappearance had passed, most of them had lost hope. In a moment, they knew, they might witness a miracle.

For cops, the face of a missing child sums up all the terrible truths they learn on the job: innocent children, just like their own, disappear every day. Despite all the prayers and all the promises, some of those little boys and girls are found dead. Even worse, many more are never found at all.

This time, though, it was going to be different. It was going to be a gift—a joyous, wondrous gift. As the detectives waited impatiently those last few seconds, hoping against hope that little Katie Beers was still alive, each made a private vow: that no one, ever, would hurt Katie Beers again.

And then they heard a child's voice. They couldn't quite make out what she was saying, but they knew: It was Katie Beers. She'd beaten the odds.

In the dungeon, one of the detectives helped Katie squeeze through the five-foot tunnel. Then he lifted her up the shaft, helping to brace her feet on the crossbeams. As she climbed to freedom Katie heard a stranger's voice. It was Andrew Siben, John Esposito's lawyer.

"Everything's going to be all right, Katie," he called down to her. "Everybody loves you. Everybody misses you. It's going to be okay."

Katie did not answer. Her head poked out of the hole, and a moment later detectives pulled her to her feet. She brushed past the roll-out stereo cabinet, a bit wobbly. Strong hands reached out to steady her. Beneath her damp clothes her skin was cold and clammy.

Katie Beers stood in John Esposito's office and searched the crowd of unfamiliar faces. The men looked so big, so serious. A few of them were smiling at her. She wanted to smile back, but she couldn't. Her legs were cramping. Her head ached. She felt nauseous, as if she were going to throw up. Later, doctors would find that she was seriously dehydrated.

In the dungeon, Katie had so often daydreamed about getting out. She had closed her eyes and imagined the celebration, the reunion with everyone she knew. But now, surrounded by strangers, sick and cold and wanting to cry, Katie Beers was frightened and upset.

Big John caught her eye, then turned away. For a moment, no one said anything at all.

"How do you feel?" a detective asked.

"I'm fine," Katie said. "How are you?"

The men smiled. Katie did too. She wrapped her thin arms around her chest and shivered.

"I'm a little cold," she said.

Oddly enough it was John Esposito who volunteered his brown suede jacket. A detective draped it around Katie's shoulders. It hung down past her knees. "Here, sit down," he said, motioning her to the couch.

There was another pause. Big John had removed the cushions from the sofa a few days earlier. He had been taking care of his sister-in-law Joanie's two German shepherds. The dogs had been chewing on the furniture.

"Just a minute," a detective said, hurrying to the next room. "It's in here."

He brought back one cushion and set it in place in the center of the sofa. He held Katie's arm gently as she sat down.

"I'm very glad to get out of there," Katie said.

Two of the detectives turned toward the door. They worked with the department's homicide division.

"This is not a homicide case," one said, smiling. "We're off the case."

One of the men picked up John Esposito's phone and immediately called D.A. Catterson. They spoke briefly. Then Sidney Siben took the phone.

"Jim, she's alive and she's safe," he said.

"Thank God," Catterson replied, sighing. "Thank God."

Katie held up a bag and pulled out the five hundred dollars Big John had given her the night before, in the bunker. She wasn't sure if it was real—or if she could keep it. At that point, Big John began to cry. To the astonishment of detectives, Katie put her hand on his shoulder.

A detective removed Katie's jacket and gave her his own blue windbreaker. He carefully raised the hood, tying it tightly under Katie's chin. It served two purposes: to keep the child warm, and to shield her face from the cameras waiting outside.

Meanwhile, a detective who had been following John Esposito from the beginning finally did what he always knew he one day would: he handcuffed the prime suspect in the disappearance of Katie Beers. John Esposito was arrested and charged with second-degree kidnapping. The charge carries a sentence of eight and a third to twenty-five years.

The detective cuffed Esposito in front. He

decided the trembling man he'd been following for two weeks was not a threat. Andrew Siben reminded his client not to talk to police. Wearing a light brown jacket and a baseball cap pulled down over his eyes, Esposito nodded.

The detective looked from Big John to little Katie. He felt the same mixed emotions he'd had from the very beginning, when he first met John Esposito. He couldn't help it: he almost liked John Esposito. But who was this man? How could he have done such an evil thing? This had been a crime of the flesh, but it was so base, so disgusting, that it was also a crime of the soul. And this frail, gentle man in front of him was the perpetrator. It was all so confusing.

Just after 2:00 P.M. on Wednesday, January 13, Katie Beers walked out of 1416 North Saxon Avenue, a few minutes before John Esposito was led to jail. She had survived 381 hours locked in the dungeon. As she got ready to walk out the door she looked at the detectives and said, softly, "Thank you for coming."

From fifty yards away, *Newsday* reporter Gary Witherspoon and several television camera operators, their Betacams on their shoulders, watched in amazement as a little girl stepped slowly down the walk and climbed into a gray unmarked Chevy. Three detectives got in with her. Laura Stone, a neighbor, saw the miracle from her doorway. "She was waving happily, like the president walking on down the road," Stone later told reporters.

The Chevy inched up the street, toward Sunrise Highway. Witherspoon leaned close to the car as it moved slowly past him.

"There she is," he murmured to himself as he made eye contact.

"Katie," he called out. "You all right?"

From the backseat, little Katie nodded.

"How do you feel?" Witherspoon asked. It was the classic reporter's question, asked usually by electronic journalists because it often got a response their minicams could record. But Witherspoon was a print journalist. He was not asking the question for the cameras. He was asking it because he really cared.

Katie smiled. She lifted her small hand and gave the burly reporter a little wave. "I feel good," she said softly. Witherspoon smiled back. He did too.

Chapter Sixteen

MARILYN BEERS and Linda Inghilleri first learned that Katie had been found from reporters sent to cover their reactions. In Mastic Beach, Marilyn Beers sat hunched over her kitchen table, chain-smoking and doodling on a piece of paper. She asked a friend of Little John's to find him. He was playing video games at Mustard's Last Stand, a teenage hangout about two miles away.

The friend, sixteen-year-old Dawn Perry, hurried off.

Marilyn said she didn't understand any of this. Not a bit. "Why would John kidnap Katie in the first place?" she asked a reporter. "I don't understand what he's saying. Why would he make this up? If he did it, I hope he's punished severely. But I don't put an accusing finger on anyone until I know for sure."

She sighed, and bent her head. The pressure was beginning to get to her. She couldn't believe Katie was really alive, not until she heard it from the police. "She's such a good kid," Marilyn said, almost in a whisper. "I do feel she's still alive. I pray to God she's alive."

For a moment there was silence. Marilyn lifted her head and looked directly at the reporter in her kitchen. "I'm sitting here dying," she said.

A detective who had arrived at the house offered Marilyn a ride to Hauppauge. Marilyn jumped up. Despite the cold winter afternoon, she left Mastic without even taking her coat. Her mother, Helen, decided the trip would be too much for her. She went next door to wait at a neighbor's house.

Dawn Perry arrived at Mustard's Last Stand out of breath. She spotted Little John at once, sitting at a table talking with his buddies.

"I need to talk to you, outside," she gasped.

Little John followed at once.

"Katie's been found," Dawn said. "She's okay."

Little John didn't wait to hear any more. He began to run.

Minutes earlier, when Teddy had heard the news, he had called John Monti, leaving a message with the psychic's wife, Kathy, telling him to hurry to the Fourth Precinct. Teddy then ran to his Plymouth Duster parked in the driveway and drove the mile east to Mill Drive. At Marilyn's door, Teddy knocked several times, peering through the little window, but Marilyn had already left.

He wondered how Marilyn had managed to get to the police station. He knew she didn't have a car.

Just as he started to pull away, he saw Little John running up. Teddy picked up his son and they sped to Hauppauge. Once they arrived, however, they waited in the lobby for hours.

By the time Marilyn Beers arrived at the Fourth Precinct, dozens of reporters and photographers had filled the lobby. Despite a driving rain, some waited outside, guarding each of the entrances and exits in order to make sure they didn't miss any of the principals in the case. After announcing herself to detectives, and being told to wait, Marilyn leaned against a rail at the side door of the precinct, smoking. Reporters pounced, quizzing her unremittingly.

How did she hear about Katie's release? Why was she now standing outside? How would this whole episode change her life?

Marilyn answered "I don't know" to most of the questions. To others, she chose not to reply at all.

A police officer caught sight of Marilyn Beers

and called out, "Your daughter's fine." A few minutes later, the door from the lobby of the precinct opened. "Want to come in?" an officer asked.

Marilyn threw her unfinished cigarette onto the sidewalk and disappeared inside.

Katie Beers had arrived at the Fourth Precinct shortly after 5:00 P.M., ushered in through a back door to the detectives' squad room, past throngs of journalists. From Esposito's house, detectives had taken her directly to a hospital just a few minutes away. There, doctors had given the child a full gynecological exam, and also took several cultures from her vagina, anus, and mouth. Hospital workers brought her a hot meal. She had a warm bath and was given new clothes. It felt good to be clean.

An unmarked police car then took her to the precinct. She was escorted to the basement, where the kidnapping task force was headquartered. Word spread throughout the precinct that until further notice no one was permitted downstairs. The lunchroom was closed. So was the weight room.

For two hours, Katie spoke to a female detective, telling her what had happened on the afternoon of December 28 and the awful days that followed. At one point, another detective fed quarters into the canteen machines outside the lunchroom and came back with potato chips and soda for the little girl.

Katie told the detective as many details as she could remember. Her upbeat manner belied the horror of what she'd been through.

It began, she explained, with the *Home Alone 2* Nintendo game. She'd perched on the edge of Big John's bed, ripped off the packaging, and together she and Big John looked over the instructions. For a few minutes they played the game. Then, without warning, Big John leaned over and started kissing her, pushing her down on the bed.

Katie had pulled away, upset. But Big John didn't stop. Katie began to push against him. Then she began to scream.

Big John panicked. He grabbed Katie and started to drag her into the small office next to his bedroom. Terrified, Katie reached for the telephone and pushed 911. Big John snatched the phone away and slammed down the receiver. Once he had her inside the office, he locked the door.

"Let me out," Katie yelled, pounding on the door. "Please, John, let me go."

As Katie continued to scream, she watched, horrified, as Big John unlocked the dungeon. When he had lifted the cement slab, he reached for her. She kicked and scratched him as hard as she could, fighting with all her might. But the little girl was no match for Big John. "Let me go," she kept screaming. "Let me *go!*"

Big John paid no attention. He pushed her down the hole and pulled her through the tunnel. At one point, he tried to explain his actions. "I'm going to kidnap you," he told her. "You have this big custody fight. You're in the middle of it. Marilyn wants you. Linda wants you. I am going to save you. No one will ever find you down here."

More than two weeks later Katie remembered the terrifying journey down the dungeon perfectly. She tried to explain it. "He started unrolling the rugs and then I was in like a cave," she told the detective. "I was in a tunnel. John was pulling me through. He said he was going to kidnap me. . . . He came down once a day with food. I asked him to come down twice a day but he said no, 'The police are on my case.' "

She stopped abruptly. "Am I going too fast for you?" she asked. "I can slow down if you want."

The detective assured Katie she was doing fine.

Katie talked about the tape recording. "He told me to make a recording to play to Aunt Linda," Katie explained. "He told me to say a man kidnapped me and he has a knife. I made another tape telling Aunt Linda Big John had me."

She also recounted the morning she watched as police searched for her. "I saw on the TV that the police were at the house," she said. "He had a camera that showed the outside. I was banging on the ceiling but they didn't hear me."

Katie told the detective about Big John's threats. "He said he would kill himself if I tried to get away," she said. "I knew if he killed himself, no one would ever find me. . . . He handcuffed me and had a chain around my neck. I couldn't move. He did this because I was banging on the ceiling."

She recounted Big John's claim just the night before that he would hang himself and leave a note pinned to his clothing, telling police how to find her. She said she had tried to convince him to let her go. "Last night I told John that I was sick and I had to see a doctor," she explained. "He said, 'You're going to have to wait,' and he left."

That night, Katie had barely slept. She kept thinking about the morning two weeks earlier when police had swarmed all over the house and couldn't find her. She had watched it on closed-circuit television, but no one had heard her screams. She tried not to wonder what would happen to her if Big John were gone. No one would have found her then.

Toward the end, the detective asked specific questions about Big John. Katie answered without hesitation. She told the police that Big John had touched her underneath her clothes about ten times over her sixteen days in the dungeon. She also said John had told her that he had a videotape of a young boy he had befriended. The video, Katie said, showed the boy "walking around with no clothes on."

On the basis of that information, police quickly submitted an affidavit for another search warrant for Esposito's home.

As Katie calmly recounted the events of the last sixteen days, pandemonium was breaking out upstairs. Linda Inghilleri had just learned that she was not permitted to see Katie.

Her emotions had been running high since a reporter stopped by that afternoon and told her there had been a break in the case.

"Please don't tell me something that's not true," Linda had cried out, nearly hysterical. "I can't let myself believe it until I hear from the police."

By 1:45 Linda's sisters had begun gathering at the house. "Thank God," her sister Carol

Stump kept murmuring. "Thank God they found her."

Sal Inghilleri chatted with reporters, pausing briefly to call Siben & Siben, looking for more information. He told reporters that he was sorry that he had trusted John Esposito. "That dirty no good—," he said. "And I stood by him all this time."

As the Inghilleris waited for official word of Katie's release, reporters asked Linda if she felt betrayed by comments from the Beers family over the last few weeks. "Yes, definitely," Linda said. "By all of them. They were giving out double messages about how they liked me."

At 2:40 P.M. the police called at last. It was confirmed: Katie was safe. Linda pointed to the Barbie Dream House, assembled on the afternoon, sixteen days earlier, that Katie had vanished. "I knew I was building that dollhouse for a reason," she said.

Linda quickly phoned her mother in West Babylon. "Mom, pick up! Mom, pick up!" she shouted into the answering machine. Ann Butler grabbed the receiver.

"What is it? What's wrong?"

A tearful Linda told her the news. Ann Butler immediately called the school bus company she worked for to say she was not coming in that afternoon. She and her son Charles raced to

Esposito's house, a few miles away. A detective in front of the house verified that Katie was alive.

"Thank God," Ann Butler said. "I want to see her. I'm going to break down doors to see her."

Back in Bay Shore, Linda had the same feeling. She asked her two sisters to wash her hair in the kitchen sink.

"I want to look as good as I feel, knowing she's coming back," she told them.

By 3:15, Linda was ready. She piled into the car with her brother, sisters, and a niece and nephew and headed to the Fourth Precinct in Hauppauge. Sal stayed home. Legally, he wasn't supposed to be near Katie. He didn't want any more problems than he already had.

As the family headed down Ocean Avenue, Linda insisted on a stop: she wanted to pick up some presents for Katie. She gave directions to a nearby stationery store and waited in the car while her siblings picked out Mickey and Minnie Mouse balloons, characters from *Beauty and the Beast*, and sugarless cinnamon chewing gum, Katie's favorite.

Linda was exuberant. "I'm happy, but I can't be completely happy until all the people who did this to Katie are all behind bars," she told her family.

Just after 4:00 P.M., Linda and her family

pulled into the back of the precinct, stopping in the middle of the police parking lot. Linda's sisters got out first and began removing Linda's wheelchair.

Inside the building, Police Officer Dave Richards, a burly, tough-talking cop with a handlebar mustache, had just returned to the station house from the scene of a bad auto accident on nearby Veteran's Memorial Highway. The misty rain that afternoon was dangerous for driving. A Suffolk County cop for twenty-six years, Richards knew that all too well.

He had just finished his shift—8:00 A.M. to 4:00 P.M.—but his relief was nowhere to be found, and his radio was once more signaling trouble. A ten-ten—another accident. This time there were fatalities involved.

Richards sighed. He was tired, but he knew he was needed back on the street. Bracing himself against the rain, he hurried past crowds of reporters positioned at the side door to the precinct. There were many other police activities going on in Hauppauge that day aside from the discovery of Katie Beers, he thought to himself.

Richards stopped short a few yards from his patrol car. His temper flared at once. A white Eldorado was blocking his path. The group of people carefully climbing out, talking loudly and animatedly, did not even notice.

Richards didn't hesitate. "Get that goddamn car out of the way," he shouted.

Linda Inghilleri's temper was equally fast-rising. "You don't understand," she snapped back, as her sisters helped her into the wheel-chair. "You don't know who I am."

"I don't give a damn who you are," Richards bellowed. "This is for police only."

"But I'm handicapped," Linda replied defiantly.

At that moment, Richards recognized the wheelchair-bound woman. He didn't care. He yelled again at the driver to move the car, and a few minutes later blasted out of the parking lot. It had been a difficult day for everyone.

Linda Inghilleri's sister wheeled her to the front of the precinct. Linda immediately sought out Dominick Varrone. "I want to see Katie, please," she told him. "She needs to see me."

Varrone, uncomfortable, edged away. "I'll see what I can do," he said, disappearing inside.

A little later another police officer broke the news to Linda. Katie was not seeing anyone, not for a while.

Linda Inghilleri's high-pitched screams ech-oed throughout the police precinct and were heard outdoors as well. Television cameras caught the commotion on tape.

"This is a rotten thing for you to do to me," she yelled, trying to wheel her way into the detectives' squad room. "I want my daughter! I want to see her, now! Give me back my daughter!"

An officer closed the door in her face.

Behind that metal door, Marilyn Beers was getting her own disturbing news: Katie was not coming home. Not yet. Officials from Suffolk County Child Protective Services pointed out that they had an extensive file on Katie Beers. Marilyn, they charged, had neglected the child in myriad ways. Mostly, she had failed to keep Katie away from John Esposito and Sal Inghilleri, even though she knew there were questions about sexual abuse.

Officials explained plainly that if Marilyn refused to sign an agreement to allow the county Department of Social Services to assume temporary custody of Katie, they would still file motions to take Katie away from her. But in that case, they said, it might then be harder for her to regain permanent custody later on.

Marilyn Beers agreed. She signed the papers, giving the county custody of Katie for the next three weeks.

As soon as she signed, a detective excused himself and went to the lobby to find Teddy.

"Marilyn needs a ride home," he said.

"Okay," Teddy said. "I'll take her."

Just after 8:00 P.M., Marilyn Beers pushed past a crush of reporters, ignoring their questions. Teddy, Little John, and John Monti were waiting.

"Let's go," she said to Teddy and Little John. Turning to Monti, she said softly, "I'm going home but I don't want the press to know. Meet me there."

The ride home to Mastic was quiet. Teddy didn't ask too many questions, and Marilyn didn't feel like talking. In the backseat, Little John was silent. He had assumed Katie would be coming home that evening. He wondered when he might see his half sister again.

John Monti was already waiting when Marilyn arrived at home. He could barely contain his curiosity.

"Well?" he said. "Did you see your child?"

"No," Marilyn said.

"What? Why didn't you see your child?"

Marilyn shrugged and turned away. "They handed me a piece of paper," she said. "They said they're going to take her either way, whether I do it the easy way or the hard way."

Monti was stunned. "Marilyn, are you serious?" he asked.

Marilyn nodded. "They could probably give her a better home than me anyway," she said.

Once again John Monti was struck by Marilyn Beers's demeanor. "She acted like she didn't even care," he said later. "No emotion. No nothing."

At the time, Monti was insistent that Marilyn fight for custody of her daughter. "You need a lawyer," he told her. "I'll get you one tomorrow."

"Okay," Marilyn Beers said. "Do what you can."

When Katie Beers emerged from the back door of the Fourth Precinct, clutching a half-eaten bag of potato chips, the media went wild. Camera lights went on, strobes started flashing, reporters began rushing at the little girl, microphones and tape recorders in hand. Flanked by a detective and a social worker from Child Protective Services, Katie only blinked. She didn't answer as reporters called out to her.

"You okay, Katie? How do you *feel?*"

Katie was taken to Schneider Children's Hospital in Queens, where she was settled into a room on the third floor. She chatted happily with the two detectives who had been with her at Esposito's house that afternoon. She asked them if she would get to go to school again; they told her she would. One of them asked her what she would wish for, if she could have three wishes.

"A thousand more wishes," came the reply.

The detective laughed. What about the next wish? he asked.

She told him she wanted to meet the rock group Kiss, the favorite band of her brother.

The two detectives remained outside Katie's hospital room door all night. It was important, they reasoned, that the little girl feel safe.

It was also important that she feel loved. Shortly after Katie arrived, several nurses got a key and raided the gift shop in the lobby. They looked over the selection of children's toys and picked out a teddy bear and a stuffed mouse. When they gave them to the little girl, she beamed. That night, little Katie Beers slept soundly for the first time in sixteen days, her new stuffed animals wrapped in her arms.

John Esposito lay on the wooden bench next to a toilet and a mirror and stared at the ceiling. He knew his family and friends were devastated. He hadn't seen them since early that morning, at Siben & Siben. He wondered what he could possibly say to them.

He thought about his mother, Rose, and how she had always fussed over him, how much she had loved her family. For the first time, Esposito was glad she wasn't alive. She could not have survived this day.

Alone in his cell that night, John Esposito wondered how things had gone so wrong. It seemed as if he'd always been Big John. Kind and generous. The perfect playmate. So many people loved him. So many children, so many grown-ups.

He alone must have known his terrible secret. Perhaps years of desire and shame had slowly worn away at his soul. The loneliness, the grief. Maybe deep down, John Esposito was as much a child as little Katie Beers.

He no longer knew himself. In his anguish, John Esposito wondered how he had become the man in the jail cell that night.

Chapter Seventeen

WORD OF KATIE'S RELEASE spread quickly. The principal at her school announced the good news over the loudspeaker. On Udall Road, shopkeepers scrawled FOUND in black markers across the Missing posters in their windows. At Spaceplex, managers toasted Katie Beers.

Yet throughout the day, officers in the public information department of the Suffolk County Police Department in Yaphank were forced to hedge on releasing information. A press release was in the works. Before it was ready, Officer Mark Ryan fielded dozens of calls from the press. "We hear she's been found," the callers would say.

Ryan remained noncommittal. "We have not been officially informed," he kept repeating.

By mid-afternoon, the release was finally ready:

> Katie Beers, the ten-year-old Mastic girl kidnapped 17 days ago, was found today by police at the home of family friend John Esposito. . . . The extent of the [damage to the] physical and mental condition of Katie Beers as a result of her ordeal has yet to be determined. She has been communicative and has been providing information to investigators in the case. She is currently in the custody of Suffolk County Child Protective Services. . . . John Esposito is being charged with kidnapping. The investigation is continuing and additional charges may be considered. He will be arraigned in First District Court, Central Islip, on January 14, 1993.

Officer Ryan typed it into a computer, printed it out, and placed it on the fax machine. "Welcome home, Katie," Ryan said as he pressed the button.

Shortly after Katie's release, attorneys at Siben & Siben met with the press. Questions came at breakneck speed. Andrew Siben did most of the talking. But his refusal to answer questions only left reporters frustrated.

"Why did Mr. Esposito do this?" one asked.

"I cannot comment on my conversation with Mr. Esposito," Siben replied.

"Does it surprise you that the police were there—living there for more than two weeks and didn't find her?"

"The story will unfold in the next few days."

"Is it fair to say that Katie had a role in her own disappearance?"

"Again, I am not going to comment on any of the details."

"Had she ever been in the Spaceplex?"

"I am not going to comment."

"Were you shocked when Mr. Esposito told you where Katie was?"

"Our concern as lawyers was to see that the child was safe."

"How long was the crawl space?"

"I cannot comment."

"How did people get into it?"

"Again, I cannot comment."

"Was she aware of this massive search for her? Did she say anything about that?"

"It is important at this time, under our attorney-client privilege, that I not disclose any information. Please. You have to bear with us." Andrew Siben was resolute; he had the best interests of his client in mind.

Then it was Sidney Siben's turn. Andrew's

partner and uncle was more loquacious. Except his spin on the story was beyond baffling. To hear him tell it, Katie Beers was perfectly content in the dungeon.

"She was fine," he told the media with a smile. "A little bruise on her knee. She was happy. Very excited. We called; we didn't hear an answer. She said, 'I'm here. I'm happy.' "

"What was Katie's reaction when she saw John Esposito?"

"She was happy when she saw him. She likes him. He's been very good to her."

"You say he's been very good to her yet he locked her in a—"

"I know," Sidney Siben said, cutting off the questioner. "But she didn't care about that."

Another reporter tried again. "Normally, a little ten-year-old would have been crying . . . , 'I want my mommy' and 'Help me.' "

Sidney Siben shook his head. "Her home conditions were such that she had more comfort and more happiness with John."

Later, a detective who spent time with Katie Beers after her release dismissed the attorney's comments. Katie, he said, was hardly happy about her days in the dungeon. "She was a very frightened little girl," he said. "She was quite upset."

* * *

By early evening, reporters hurried to the next press conference. It was held at 5:30 in the second-floor auditorium of a county building next door to the Fourth Precinct. On hand were Police Commissioner Peter Cosgrove, Lieutenant Dominick Varrone, and several other detectives.

Varrone described the dungeon, and how Esposito had managed to keep it concealed. The detective was quick to praise his department's tenacity.

"I think the combined effort of all involved, to include the intense pressure that we had on Mr. Esposito, including constant police presence, constant police surveillance . . . We can only speculate what his motives may have been but I think at some point in time he altered whatever his intent was."

Varrone opened the floor to questions. Several reporters spoke at once.

"What do you think his ultimate goal was, Lieutenant?"

"I can only guess at this point."

"Can you give us a guess?"

"I don't think his intentions were good. Obviously to have a ten-year-old girl secreted in this manner, against her will . . . we understand at times chained around the neck. It's absolutely bizarre, it's an incredible sequence of events. We are very fortunate that she is alive."

"Lieutenant, do you have reason to believe that anyone else in the family or friends may have been involved because of this supposed custody battle?"

"At this point we do not. I want to add that apologies are forthcoming to the family. We were pretty tough on them. We pushed them around, so to speak. We didn't trust any of them."

Then came the question that Lieutenant Varrone had been expecting all day, ever since he learned where Katie Beers had been for the last sixteen days. He knew the department was going to take heat for not finding Katie sooner. After all, they had searched the Esposito compound again and again and never found the child—even though she was there all the time.

The question was long and wordy. "Lieutenant, do you have any apologies for anybody else, knowing that there was a state and national search, and you had men in that house searching, in the words of the attorney, tearing the place apart, and the girl was there all the time? Are you embarrassed by this?"

Varrone did not hesitate. "Absolutely not," he said. "I think when you become aware of the manner in which this person was secreted, the only possible way this person would be found would be by the individual coming forth and telling us, or it may take a partial demolition of the building to get to where she was secreted."

It was—and remained—a touchy issue. In fact, D.A. Catterson and Police Commissioner Cosgrove had gotten into at least one shouting match over it. Catterson had demanded to know how detectives could have searched the suspect's apartment three times without finding the dungeon.

The police had been fooled, but at the same time their methodology had worked. The little girl had been found. The press conference was over.

Shortly before 6:00 A.M. the next day, a fax came through at Weinisch's Deli in Smithtown, less than two miles from the Fourth Precinct. Owner Artie Weinisch picked up the paper and scanned the printed list of names. He called out to his wife, Debbie.

"Hey, look at this," he said, waving the paper. "They've got John Esposito. We get to make his breakfast."

Debbie flipped the eggs frying on the grill. For about a decade, Weinisch's Deli had been cooking breakfast for all the prisoners in holding cells at the Fourth Precinct. By 6:30 A.M. a police officer would arrive to pick up the meals. The menu was always the same: fried egg sandwiches on a roll, and coffee with milk. No sugar was permitted; a prisoner might be allergic.

The list of names of those arrested the night before came in every morning like clockwork. For the Weinisches, however, this one was special. Artie and Debbie had been following the Katie Beers story in the press; they had been predicting all along that they would see the name John Esposito on that list one day. Artie took a felt-tip pen and circled it. At last Katie's captor had been caught.

Breakfast was served to John Esposito shortly after 7:00 A.M. Not long after, Police Officer Dave Richards reported for his daytime shift. He wasn't sure what he'd be assigned to, but it hardly mattered. Richards walked the beat, working nights, weekends—a changing schedule that didn't do much for his family life. But he had to admit it; he loved being a cop.

"You have prisoners today, okay?" Lieutenant Paul Herrle told him.

"Fine," said Richards.

"You have Esposito this morning," Herrle added.

Richards shrugged. He walked by the holding cell and shook his head. The place smelled horribly. "B.O.," Richards said to himself. "Ugh!" During the night, Esposito had gotten a roommate in the next cell: a Suffolk man who had been drinking heavily and was charged with beating his elderly father. For a moment Richards wondered why the cops on duty hadn't closed the outside door to the holding cell as they usually did.

Then he remembered: John Esposito was on a suicide watch.

Richards saw Esposito sitting quietly on the bench. On a tray was his breakfast, untouched.

"You didn't drink your coffee," Richards said.

"There's no sugar," Esposito answered softly.

"Sugar is no good for you," said Richards, his face deadpan. "Sugar makes you too sweet."

Officer Richards turned to the other cell. "What are you in here for?" he asked.

"I had a fight with my father," the man answered.

Richards didn't say anything. Disgusted, he walked out.

He poked his head out of the side door of the precinct, surveying the crowd of reporters and photographers. A police spokesman was already on the steps, explaining what would happen when Esposito was brought out to the police van, on his way to court for arraignment.

Ordinarily, prisoners on a "perp walk" are chained to each other and led to the van. This time, the police agreed to make it easier on the press. They would bring Esposito out last, alone. To help photographers get a clear shot, the police van would wait on the opposite side of the parking lot instead of the usual place, in front of the door.

"We don't want you to rush at him," the cops told photographers. "We know what you need. We'll make sure you get it."

The photographers were relieved. Still, they were impatient as they waited for John Esposito.

Inside, Katie's captor was trembling. Richards and Police Officer George Reading led him out of the holding cell and down the hallway toward the exit.

Esposito turned to the cops. "I'm scared," he whispered. "I'm going to get killed."

Richards looked down at Esposito. What a little guy, he thought. He couldn't help but feel sorry for him.

"Don't worry, nothing's going to happen to you," Richards said firmly. "I got you."

As they reached the door, Reading couldn't contain his curiosity.

"Hey, who built that bunker?" he asked.

"I did," Esposito said softly.

Seconds later, when the three men stepped outside, camera shutters snapped wildly. They walked slowly down the steps. Every few seconds, Richards and Reading paused to allow photographers to get a clear shot of John Esposito. Reporters called out questions.

"Good morning, Mr. Esposito. How are you?"

"Don't say nothin'," Richards whispered to Esposito. He didn't. He was quiet all the way to the van.

It was just a few miles to the courthouse. Within minutes, Richards pulled over and led the prisoner inside. He handed him over to court guards and watched him take a seat on a bench in a holding cell, alone. Richards's assignment was over. Before he left, however, he couldn't resist a gentle taunt.

The cop walked over to the bars. "Hey," he called out to Esposito, motioning. "Come here."

John Esposito obeyed. Richards leaned toward him. Esposito moved forward to hear.

"You have a rainbow day," the cop whispered in his ear.

John Esposito did not say a word.

Chapter Eighteen

JOHN ESPOSITO'S ARRAIGNMENT lasted less than ten minutes. In a dark suit and tie, Esposito appeared ashen and unshaven in front of Judge Patrick Barton in courtroom D-11 on the fourth floor of District Court in Central Islip.

The court clerk introduced case No. 844-93.

"People versus John Esposito. New arrest, Judge. Felony. Kidnapping in the second degree."

The assistant district attorney, William Ferris, spoke first.

"Your Honor, the defendant is charged with kidnapping in the second degree. It is a very serious offense. It is a violent felony. The defendant if convicted on this stands to be incarcerated from eight and a third to twenty-five years. The case is very strong. There has been much media attention on this case and the People are going forth strenuously with his prosecution."

Ferris glanced at his notes. "Your Honor, we are going to ask the court to hold this defendant without bail in this matter. I want to let the court know that the case we have is very strong. . . . [Katie Beers] was found in a subterranean vault underneath [Esposito's] house. . . . The defendant knew what was going on. He even went to the police publicly saying he wished to find Katie. . . . I am going to ask therefore that the defendant be held without any bail."

Now it was Andrew Siben's turn. The attorney did his best. He told the judge that John Esposito was a lifelong resident of Bay Shore and a contractor by trade. He pointed out that except for an incident many years earlier, John Esposito had no prior criminal history. Siben added that members of Esposito's family were in the courtroom, that they loved and supported John completely.

But mostly Andrew Siben stressed John Esposito's conduct the previous day. The defendant, he maintained, had acted courageously: he had freed Katie Beers. Surely that must count for something.

"Your Honor, rather than going into the actual details of this case, I can honestly say that

Mr. Esposito was instrumental in the recovery of Katie Beers," Siben said. "Katie Beers might not be alive if Mr. Esposito did not cooperate. Mr. Esposito has shown a sense of responsibility and compassion by not fleeing when he had the opportunity to do so. He is not a threat to anyone within the community. . . . Your Honor, without the help of Mr. Esposito this mystery might not ever have been solved."

Siben's argument did not sit well with William Ferris. The assistant district attorney cut in to emphasize a closing point: "Your Honor, in terms of mystery—there was no mystery that Katie Beers for a two-week period of time was secreted in his house," he said.

Ferris's argument was convincing. It took only a few moments for Judge Barton to render his decision: He ordered John Esposito held on half a million dollars' bail. The judge then granted Siben's request that Esposito be held in protective custody and be permitted counseling sessions. Later that morning, John Esposito was moved to the Suffolk County Correctional Facility in Riverhead, about forty miles east. As he was led to his cell, other inmates jeered and shouted profanities. John Esposito wondered what they would do to him if they had the chance.

That morning, John Monti drove Marilyn to Bridgehampton, about thirty-five miles east of

Mastic, to meet with John Jiras, a tall, white-haired attorney with a practice on Suffolk's East End.

"You'll like Jiras," Monti told her. "He's very aggressive."

The three met for several hours. Surprisingly, Jiras had heard little of Katie Beers, but he knew a high-profile case when he saw one. It didn't take him long to hold a news conference. He summoned reporters to the home of Teddy Rodriguez that afternoon.

Jiras told reporters that he doubted Marilyn's agreement to put Katie in the temporary care of Suffolk County authorities was legally binding. Marilyn had signed the agreement, he argued, while under grave emotional duress. "The truth is that the natural mother is the most suitable person to have the child," he said. "Marilyn Beers wasn't advised properly."

Marilyn was in tears. "Put yourself in my shoes," she said. "How would you feel if somebody took your child away, and then she was found, and then the county took her away?"

By midmorning, a large crowd had gathered in front of 1416 North Saxon Avenue. Bright yellow police ribbons cordoned off the main house and the converted garage. Behind the barrier neighbors assembled in small groups, telling reporters what they knew of John Esposito. He was kind. Gentle. Loving toward children, they all said. Such a nice family. Such a shame.

Some local teenagers, however, were less sympathetic. One young man who delivered Esposito's newspapers halfheartedly grumbled that Esposito owed him for the past week's deliveries. "Not that I'll ever see that money now," he cracked.

Others poked fun at Esposito's delicate manner. "You could tell by the way he shook hands," one young man commented, exaggerating a limp handshake. "He was like a girl."

Phil Vollaro, seventeen, who lived down the block, recalled tossing a football with Esposito and occasionally playing Nintendo games in the rec room of the converted garage.

"We all thought he was weird," Vollaro said. "He was nice but he'd have mood swings and walk out of the house and cover his face. We didn't know what was going on. We just knew he was sometimes weird."

As reporters collected tidbits on John Esposito, police officers combed the area. It had been a busy night. Shortly after Katie's release, the Suffolk County Police Department's I.D. bureau had sent about six of its specialists, including a supervisor, to the house. Most had been working nonstop through the night. Using a camcorder, camera experts had recorded exactly what it entailed to unlock Katie's prison.

This morning, however, detectives had another important project—to investigate the possibility that other children had been held, perhaps killed, in John Esposito's bunker. Trained dogs hunted the area, and detectives painstakingly detailed each discovery plucked from the bunker. *Newsday* printed a long list of what they found:

horizontal tunnel
nightgown
eight pairs of panties
Play Skool baby monitor
three swabs of stains
broken pieces of handcuff
handcuffs
urinary drainage bag
hand massager
box of Big Brothers business-type cards
video monitor
video surveillance manual
assorted cassette recorders
assorted video cassettes
8-millimeter movie camera
videocassette: *The Will of John Esposito*
switchblade knives

Marlin model 60 .22-cal. rifle
carpentry tools

Also uncovered were stacks of photographs of children. None of the pictures, detectives later revealed, turned out to be pornographic.

By afternoon, reporters were getting restless—and cold. Many of them had been camped out in front of the house since 9:00 A.M. They'd talked enough to locals. It was time for the police to do the talking: the previous day's press conference hadn't answered enough of the media's questions.

Around 2:00 P.M., Sergeant Kevin Fallon of the public information office introduced Lieutenant Varrone and Clint Van Zandt, a supervising agent for the FBI's behavioral science lab in Quantico, Virginia. Television cameras trained on the two men as they stepped up to a makeshift podium in front of the Esposito house.

"Mr. Van Zandt, a lot of people have said this has a similarity to *The Silence of the Lambs*," asked a print reporter. "What do you say about that?"

"I think it does," Van Zandt responded. "It's out of *Silence of the Lambs*, but it's much more sophisticated. In the movie you've got this hole dug in the ground and you've got Buffalo Bill keeping somebody in the hole. This is a much higher level of sophistication, as far as being able to conceal it. It was a prison from medieval times. I've never seen anything in all my years as elaborate as this. This thing was like out of a horror movie."

Van Zandt didn't wait for the next question. He quickly addressed the biggest controversy surrounding the case: Why hadn't the police been able to locate Katie?

"As far as 'Should they have found it?'—that's a legitimate question that you all have," he told the crowd. "I asked myself the same thing: How do you miss something like that?"

But Van Zandt insisted this case was unique. He pointed out how well concealed the dungeon was, and how unusual it was that a missing child was actually sequestered—alive—in the suspect's home.

"If someone told you that room was there I'd put money on the line you'd have to tear that house apart to find it," he said. "It was so well concealed and so well constructed. It is so totally unusual to find something like that. It is absolutely reasonable that a trained law enforcement agency could go in and really shake that house, looking in all the obvious and not-so-obvious places, and not find it. The only thing that broke this case was the tenacity of the police department and the FBI not quitting. They kept putting pressure on the prime suspect."

Reporters' queries did not diminish. Journalists promptly turned to the pedophilia issue: Had John Esposito sexually abused Katie Beers? What, if anything, had happened in the dungeon on those nights he brought her food?

Pressed by the media, Van Zandt agreed to talk about pedophilia—in general. But the behavioral expert carefully avoided mentioning John Esposito's name.

"If you have someone in their thirties, in their forties, and you see that they have had some contact with a child—if you see a past history of attempted kidnapping, sexual assault—normally you do not see someone at that age where this would be the first time," he said. "There would be a past history of something like that. The question that has to be resolved here is that a lot of people don't take an action past a fantasy. You and I may fantasize about building a sailboat. And once we've built the sailboat, that's it—we don't necessarily have to sail it. But there are other people who build the sailboat because they plan on sailing across the ocean in it, and they're going to use it. And I think the analogy is here. And that's what I see these [law enforcement] agencies still doing on a twenty-four-hour basis—trying to answer the questions you're asking. Was this room used before? Has anyone else been contained in it?"

In dealing with pedophilia, Van Zandt explained, there are two extremes. "You can have someone go out on the street, kidnap a child, sexually assault them, and either they turn them loose or kill them. The opposite extreme is someone who spends weeks, months, or years cultivating that child, bringing them along, lavishing them with gifts, friendship, meals, sometimes gifts for the family. And then, as that cultivation period goes on, there then becomes the sexual relationship between the adult and the child. And it comes on such a gradual level. Normally, as the sexual relationship increases, so do the gifts. Young children just cannot differentiate. It's come on so gradual. They feel, 'If I go home and tell Mom and Dad what Uncle Louie did, then I'm going to lose the presents and lose the friendship.' And then if you take children, especially someone from a lower economic group that's not used to the lavishness of these gifts, they don't want to lose that. So they separate themselves: 'This is the person who enjoys the gifts and enjoys the friendship, and this is part of me that doesn't like what's taking place. I don't like what Uncle

So-and-so is doing to me, but it's a short period of time. The larger period of time is we have fun together. We play games together.' When you're balancing the two, especially when you're a child, you want the fun. You do away with the other."

A few miles away, in his office at Spaceplex, Gary Tuzzalo was going over the amusement center's finances. Ever since John Esposito announced that a little girl had vanished from Spaceplex, business had fallen significantly. Fewer parents dropped their children off while they shopped in nearby malls. Even requests for birthday parties were down. Tuzzalo and his partners wondered if now things might turn around. Would the children return?

They had worked hard to open Spaceplex. The amusement center's employees were well trained and friendly. The place was sparkling clean. As for safety, it was a point of pride for Gary Tuzzalo: security was always tight. All that work appeared to have made a difference: Spaceplex had been successful ever since its opening two years earlier.

Leaning back in his chair, Tuzzalo thought about the previous night. He'd been at work when a friend called to tell him the good news.

"Did you hear Katie was found?" the friend had said. "She's alive."

"That's terrific," Tuzzalo had said. "I knew it was a hoax the whole time. I knew she was never here. I'm glad we've been exonerated."

"Congratulations, Gary," the friend said.

For the next few hours, dozens of calls had flooded Spaceplex, from friends and customers. Word spread quickly among the amusement center's managers and security guards as well.

"Gary, that's great," everyone had said. "We knew it couldn't happen at Spaceplex. This place is too safe."

Gary Tuzzalo had closed his eyes. It was hard to concentrate. All he could think of was Katie. He'd seen the news reports as Katie emerged from the police station, her little face practically lost in that oversized blue hood. He remembered her panicked voice on Linda Inghilleri's answering machine. Tuzzalo thought about those long days and nights in John Esposito's dungeon. Suddenly, he had an idea. He spent the rest of the day calling his six business partners.

"Whenever she's ready," he had told each of them, "Spaceplex is going to throw Katie Beers the best birthday party she's ever had."

The next day, Friday, Katie Beers met with a grand jury in Suffolk County. She didn't want to go, she told detectives. "I don't want to talk about what happened to me," she said earnestly.

It was necessary, they explained. Katie finally agreed. She testified in private with no one present except an assistant district attorney, a court stenographer and the 21-member grand jury. She was neither afraid, nor shy. And she answered every question put before her.

After her testimony, Katie met with DA James Catterson. He held out his hand, completely engulfing her tiny hand in his mammoth paw.

He smiled at her and she smiled back. But she had something on her mind. There was something she wanted to get straight—fast.

"You know, my name is really Katherine," she said.

The DA nodded. "Katherine," he repeated. He promised to remember to call her Katherine.

Katie told him she wanted to write the story of her life some day. She said the name on the cover would be Katherine Marie Beers. "It would look good on a book jacket," she said.

The DA agreed. It certainly would.

Earlier, Katie had learned that she would be going to a foster home in East Hampton, about half an hour east of Mastic Beach. The family, she was told, was very nice. They lived near the beach and had a friendly dog and a big backyard. There was a boy just her age. Best of all, she would get to go to school again.

Meanwhile, Marilyn Beers spent Friday in Family Court with her new attorney. At this point, the best she could hope for was a visit with her daughter. She had still not seen her, even though Katie had been out of the dungeon for two days. The county social workers were against any visit, but Jiras fought hard.

Around 7 P.M., a compromise was reached. Katie was brought to a county building in Central Islip for a brief reunion with her mother. When she saw Marilyn, Katie ran to her and jumped into her arms, wrapping her skinny legs around her mother's ample waist.

"I love you," Katie said, beginning to cry. "I love you. I love Grandma. I love Little John."

"I love you, too," Marilyn whispered. "Don't worry. You'll be home soon."

Then the visit was over. It had been emotional for both mother and daughter. And they did not talk about John Esposito at all.

Chapter Nineteen

NATIONAL ATTENTION to the Katie Beers case grew swiftly. The story of the little girl's plight was broadcast on network news, and made the front pages of newspapers as far away as London and Los Angeles. Diane Sawyer did a segment on *Prime Time Live.* And talk show hosts Phil Donahue, Maury Povich, and Montel Williams devoted entire programs to the story.

The war between the Inghilleris and the Beerses made for high ratings. A day after Katie was released from the dungeon, Donahue aired a segment featuring Linda Inghilleri, talking from her home, via satellite. In the show's midtown Manhattan studio were her brother, Charlie Butler, her nephew, John Stump, and Katie's grandmother, Helen Beers. Standing by helplessly in the wings, wishing he could have gone on too, was Little John. Because he was only sixteen, the program's lawyers said he needed permission from his mother.

On the show, Linda insisted that she, not Marilyn, had raised Katie. And she attacked Marilyn for using her mother, Helen Beers, simply to get money and baby-sitting services. It wasn't a fair fight; the aging Helen Beers was hardly the match of the volatile Linda.

"Mrs. Beers, your daughter was abusing you," she said. "I once even called adult protective services to protest—"

"I don't know what you're talking about," said Helen, looking confused.

"When your daughter wanted four hundred dollars to fix her car, I told you it cost a hundred and fifty. I said, 'She needs extra pocket money. Mrs. Beers, wake up,' and you still . . . I could show it right to you in front of your face, you still wouldn't admit it, like you're doing today on TV. . . . I showed you all the TVs, VCRs, clothes, and it was right in front of your face, but you still wouldn't accept the fact what your daughter was doing to you."

"I don't—I was thinking about something else right now," Helen said faintly.

Linda kept going. "When you were getting billed from American Express and MasterCard from hotels and restaurants—"

"Oh, wait a minute," Helen broke in.

Phil Donahue took back the floor, changing the subject with a wave of the hand. He brought up the squalid years in the Higbie Drive house in West Islip. "Helen, they're saying your house was a dump."

"That isn't true."

"They're saying your house was a wreck—there were things all over the floor. It was dirty."

Helen tried to explain. "So when you have children and everything—they were living there with three dogs one time—"

"A few rats," cut in John Stump.

"—just two years ago," Helen continued. "Linda's calling me upstairs to clean up the dog mess all the time. My telephone bill—I still owe the telephone company a thousand dollars, which I never, ever, used the phone. . . . Linda was using it from the upstairs."

For the next hour, Linda and her relatives continued to accuse Marilyn and her mother of being unfit to raise Katie. Helen Beers tried in vain to defend herself and her daughter. At one point, however, it was Linda who was on the defensive. Donahue questioned her about the sex abuse charges facing her husband, Sal. Linda refused to comment.

"I came on this show today because I feel what the paper has printed, what the news people have said, is nothing to the truth," she announced. "The truth of the matter is that I have done my best for Katie. I have contacted all the right authorities when there was a problem. I took care of everything step by step and my main concern is Katie, and I want her back, and even if I could just hold her for a minute is all I want, and then my life will be happy, and I know there will be a better road to come."

At the end, Linda spoke directly into the camera. "I just want to say to Katie, I love you, Katie. I'll never stop loving you, I'll never stop helping you and get you to where you want to be. I love you, Katie."

Donahue's show earned a high rating—10.9. Meanwhile, other talk shows were gearing up to air their own segments. Maury Povich's executive producer, Diane Rappoport, and his producer Liz Frillici, spent the entire weekend following Katie's release trying to set up an interview with Marilyn Beers. From her home in Connecticut, Frillici checked in with Rappoport in Manhattan every few hours with updates.

Frillici first contacted Marilyn's lawyer, John Jiras, and her psychic, John Monti, hoping they'd persuade her to go on the show. Finally, the producer spoke directly to Marilyn.

"Listen, we've heard and read everything about you in all the newspapers and you're telling us you're being crucified in the papers and no one's getting the story straight," said Frillici. "We're going to give you the opportunity to tell your story."

Frillici made an offer: "Listen, this is what we'll do," she said. "We'll bring you to New York. You'll meet Maury. You'll see if you're comfortable with the show."

Marilyn agreed. Meanwhile, the show's producers tried to convince Linda Inghilleri to go on as well. Linda said she would—for a price. The show's producers turned her down. They did not pay for interviews, they explained.

On Monday, a limousine arrived at 80 Mill Drive in Mastic Beach just after 9:00 A.M. Several other limousines were parked by the house already. Producers from rival talk shows were busy trying to lure the Beerses to appear on their own shows.

Back in Manhattan, Rappoport was on edge. She called the driver to make sure things were going smoothly.

"Are they in the car yet?" she asked.

"No," the driver replied. "They went to buy cigarettes."

Rappoport cringed. "I have cigarettes waiting for them here," she moaned. "Just get them here."

Shortly before 10:00 A.M., Marilyn, Little John, Jiras, and Monti climbed into the limousine and headed for Manhattan. As they pulled away from Mill Drive, the other limousines quickly followed.

When the Beers group arrived at the studio, entering through a back door in the garage, they were brought to a conference room to meet with Maury Povich and his staff. They talked for about an hour.

"You're here to tell your story—that's what we want," Povich told Marilyn. "You've got a whole hour to tell it. It's never been heard before."

Outside reporters had already gathered. The Povich staff quickly realized it wouldn't be difficult for the press to find out where the Beers group was staying: at the end of the show, a trailer always aired the announcement, "Guests of the Maury Povich show stay at the Lowes Hotel."

The staff decided to plan a ruse. They booked the family into another hotel, and then sent a group of young interns to take the limousine for a drive, to shake off anyone following the Beerses. Then they called a private taxicab company, and sent the Beerses to a different hotel.

The next day, the Beerses relaxed in a greenroom just off the studio before the taping. John Jiras seemed to be enjoying himself. He made nonstop phone calls to tell friends to be sure to watch him on television. Although Jiras had worked as a makeup artist, he surprised the Maury Povich staff by refusing any makeup. A few worried makeup artists tried to convince him his face would look shiny, but he still declined.

Maury Povich opened the show with these words: "We have a New York story that is so big it has pushed the bombing of Iraq and Bill Clinton's inaugural off the front pages. It's a big story about a little girl. Her name is Katie Beers. . . . They are calling Katie Beers's kidnapping worse than a real-life *Silence of the Lambs* and here's why."

Film footage showed the dungeon, what Povich called "a passage to perversion." Then came the tearstained face of John Esposito, begging for Katie's safe return. Finally there was Katie, emerging from the Fourth Precinct in her big windbreaker, clutching the bag of potato chips.

"After you watched where Katie was buried for sixteen days, how do you feel?" he asked Marilyn.

"Can I bury him in there?" Marilyn snapped.

"Did you know Katie was spending a lot of time with John Esposito?"

"No, I did not."

"Why are you here?"

"Because of my daughter."

"You're very uncomfortable," Povich noted. "You don't want to be here, but you're doing it for your daughter."

Marilyn nodded. "There's been a lot of stories going on," she said. "The papers have been crucifying me, and I don't think it's right."

Marilyn went on to say how she filed sex

abuse charges against John Esposito a year earlier, and she boasted that Katie was thrilled to see her. "The best way to describe it—she saw me, yelled 'Mommy,' and flew into my arms and wouldn't leave my arms for the rest of the visit."

Povich turned to Little John.

"What was your relationship with John?" he asked.

"We were just good friends."

"Why was he a friend?"

"He was nice to hang around with. We always went out to stores, trips, all sorts of stuff."

Did he ever abuse you?

"Yes, he did . . . He sexually molested me in ways . . . I'm not getting into it."

After the commercial, John Jiras tried to explain the dynamics of sexual abuse. "Let's set the whole record straight—about a young kid six and seven years old, and there's a guy giving him candy, stereos, and this guy giving him whatever he gives him," he said. "It's like your father catching you masturbating: You're not going to run and say, 'Guess what happened to me today.' You're going to hide that. You're going to suppress that. All psychiatrists will tell you that."

A woman from the audience waved her hand. "You have really used bad judgment in raising this child," she told Marilyn.

Marilyn flinched. "Most of my life I have

worked anywhere between twelve, eighteen, and twenty-four hours a day. My average week was eighty-two hours a week."

"You have to understand that she's a single parent," Jiras added.

Another question from the audience. "Where is Katie's father?"

Marilyn Beers spoke matter-of-factly. "He is unknown," she said. "I don't know who he is. I was out drinking one night and it just happened. So crucify me. I don't believe in abortion."

At the end of the taping, Rappoport was surprised at the audience's hostility. The show was scheduled to air on Wednesday, but the presidential inauguration interfered. Rappoport arranged the segment for Thursday, worrying the whole time that Marilyn might talk to a rival in the meantime.

Little John enjoyed himself immensely. "I'll come back if you need an update," he told the producers.

A few days later, Montel Williams aired a segment on Katie Beers. On it, Linda Inghilleri spoke once again via satellite.

"I raised her," she said. "I taught her how to talk. I potty trained her. I put her in her first bed. I was with her when she was sick. I was up all night. Marilyn is the biological mother but I'm the mother who nurtured Katie."

"Linda, what do you think should happen to Mr. Esposito?"

"My feelings to John Esposito is that what comes around goes around and he will get what he deserves."

Linda tried to fend off criticisms that she looked the other way when it came to John Esposito. "Well, he had a split personality that nobody knew about," she said. "If he could fool the police—he had her right under their feet—look how well he fooled us."

She made her case for having Katie turned over to her.

"To me there is no difference between John Esposito and Marilyn Beers," she said. "They both have claimed to love her but in a sick way. John had her living *under* a garage and Marilyn had her living *in* a garage. They have both shared the same fake tears. But Katie and I have shared a real love, a real home, and real tears to be together forever. Katie has always been my number one priority."

"Your husband has been accused of sexually molesting Katie," Williams said.

Linda nodded. "Just like everybody else out there, I want the mystery to all this solved, too."

Chapter Twenty

UNTIL NOW, Springs, a tiny hamlet (pop. 4,350) in the township of East Hampton, was best known for its great artists. Such talents as Jackson Pollock and Willem de Kooning have lived there, drawn by its rural isolation, its proximity to New York City, and its great light. The area is bounded on three sides by the water that lies between the two forks of eastern Long Island.

On January 16 Springs became Katie Beers's home, at least temporarily. She moved into a foster home in a large brown shingled house with a gray shingled roof that looks more like a house on Cape Cod than one in the suburbs of New York City. It has two white benches built into the sides of the front porch, and two white columns by the front door. The adjoining garage has a second story and all the earmarks of a furnished apartment above the car level.

Near the road is a basketball court; in the fenced-in backyard is a swimming pool and a golden retriever. Clothes hang on the line, for this is a house with many children. There are two girls, seventeen and fourteen, and two boys, ten and two. The ten-year-old is a foster child, for this is also a family that understands that children can suffer through no fault of their own. Indeed, Katie's new foster mother was adopted herself as a child.

Her foster father is a county corrections officer, working at the Riverhead jail. A decorated Vietnam vet, he is known to play basketball with local kids. His interest is so great that several years ago he spoke before the East Hampton Town Board to condemn a town policy of ripping down basketball nets on road shoulders. One eighth-grader recalls that last summer the foster father took half the neighborhood to Indian Wells Beach in Amagansett.

On her first weekend with her new foster family, Katie got her hair permed. The family took her out to dinner at a local Chinese restaurant. She also got her own room. No more sharing a single bed with her mother or Aunt Lin.

Katie quickly learned that life was very different there. She had a set bedtime and had to take a daily bath. She played with the home computer. Her foster family did not allow her to watch the news or read the papers. And on her first day of school, her foster mother made her a hot breakfast. No one had ever served her breakfast before, she told her foster mom.

If Katie had a new world to learn, her foster family had a new person to understand as well. Katie was not like a lot of young people. Her food choices sometimes were unexpected. How many ten-year-olds in America ever ask for brussels sprouts?

On Tuesday, January 19, six days after her release from John Esposito's dungeon, Katie joined Dolores McGintees's fourth-grade class at Springs School, a kindergarten-through-eighth-grade pink and white school on School Street off Springs-Fireplace Road in East Hampton. It is about a mile and a half from her new home and Katie goes by bus or catches a ride with her foster parents. Oddly enough, she passes Higbie Street on her way, but this is a far different world from the one she knew in West Islip.

She never goes to school alone. She is escorted both ways by her foster brothers and sisters. Once she is at school, officials make sure she is in the company of at least one other student at all times. No one is sure what adverse reactions she might have after the ordeal she has been through.

Indeed, all of East Hampton seems to be looking out after her. Before she ever arrived, Police Chief Thomas Scott, who runs the fifty-member police department on Pantigo Road, received a call that Katie was going to be staying with a local foster family. He promptly put out an advisory to all personnel on Thursday, January 14, the day after Katie was found. Marked CONFIDENTIAL, his memo said:

> Please be advised that Katie Beers will be residing at [address deleted]. [Name deleted] is concerned that the media will be around his residence and wants the police department to be aware of this. It appears that Miss Beers will be attending Springs School as of Monday, January 18, 1993. It is not known how long she will be in our area.
>
> I realize that this information will become public at some point in time. The police department will *not* be the agency to release the information.

Katie's first day of school was uneventful. Afterwards, she brought a new friend home to play.

Her second day of school was considerably different. An effusive James Catterson, the district attorney of Suffolk County, told reporters all about Katie's new foster home and foster family. It took no time at all for reporters to figure out what school she was attending. When an unmarked sheriff's car drove her to class that day, there were at least three camera crews waiting to film her.

Then WLNG-AM/FM, a radio station in nearby Sag Harbor, made things worse. It announced the name of Katie's school.

Joe Ricker, news director of WLNG, got a call from his daughter, Dina, around 7:30 A.M. She and her husband, David, live in Springs.

"David was down by Springs School," Dina said. "He said TV cameras were there because Katie Beers is going to be enrolled in the school."

"How do you know?"

"David called and told me. Someone told him."

"I appreciate it," her father said. "Let me check it out."

He called Springs School but the line was busy. So he called the Associated Press. It confirmed that the three network stations—WABC, WCBS, and WNBC—had all sent camera crews to the school.

So Ricker announced it on his next newscast, about 8:45 A.M. "TV cameras are there from New York City," he told his listeners. "We understand from reliable sources that Katie Beers is at Springs School and living in the Springs area."

That brought even more reporters. Students were told not to talk to the press. And that afternoon, a red-faced Catterson held a press conference in Riverhead, pleading with news organizations not to release the name of Katie's foster family. He held up a sign: GIVE KATHERINE A CHANCE.

East Hampton police were more direct. At 3:00 P.M. Lieutenant John Claflin announced that Katie had left the building and that anyone trespassing on school property would be arrested. And Chief Scott circulated another memo, also marked CONFIDENTIAL.

> The press is aware that Katie Beers is going to Springs School. I know certain reporters are aware of where she is residing. Be alert for any member of her family (or other persons mentioned by the media) who may be in the area.
>
> If you observe any of these people please notify your supervisor who will contact either Captain Segelken or myself.
>
> Please be reminded that you are to give no information to the press.

That day, reporters from New York City's four dailies began calling the *East Hampton*

Star, trying to find out about the foster family. The *New York Post* was especially tenacious, calling at least five times and sending a reporter to the newspaper's newsroom at 9:30 that night, asking to see a galley of its next day's story.

"The hell with them," said a reporter. "Why should we give it to him? Let him wait until tomorrow."

That night, Katie's foster father called the *Star*, cautioning the person on the other end of the line not to call him by name because he was using a cellular phone and it was easily bugged.

He complained that the newspapers had sent reporters to ask his neighbors about him. He said he had not yet had time to tell them that Katie was staying with his family.

"I'd like to tell them myself, before someone comes pounding on the doors."

Reporter Rick Murphy later spoke to Katie's foster mother. "We don't intend on using your name," he said.

"Thank you," she said.

The paper also decided to hold back on its future stories. "We decided not to do a Katie Beers update every week," Murphy said in an interview. "When it's all over we'll do an interview with them. . . . What are we going to do, get her coming out of the house with a lunch box?"

The next day, Katie's third day in school, the *East Hampton Star* ran a front-page story headlined A NEW LIFE FOR KATIE. In the story it reported that the radio station had leaked the news.

That prompted a testy phone call from Joe Ricker, who denied the station had been the first to leak the name of Katie's school.

The following week, Ricker wrote a letter to the editor of the *East Hampton Star*.

> Your front-page story this week on Katie Beers leads your readers to assume that WLNG not only took the wraps off Katie's new location, but that we singularly broke the embargo on identifying the location. WLNG News did not announce her new location until the day after New York City TV clearly identified her new school on the evening news. By then the wraps were off and her new location became common knowledge—thanks to New York City TV. Any secrecy about Katie's location faded with the evening news.
>
> We have a 30-year history of respecting confidences, any embargo and sensitive news story. We have never taken that re-

sponsibility lightly. A check with any local police department or government agency will bear us out. Your jab at WLNG should have been aimed at New York City TV. But, maybe your arms are too short to box with the Big Apple boys.
Joe Ricker
News Director
WLNG-AM/FM

The *Star* gave its response in the same issue:

The *Star* was not casting blame. Secrets don't last long in small communities. WLNG broke the news that Katie Beers was living in and going to school in Springs on Wednesday morning, Jan. 20. The New York City TV program to which Mr. Ricker refers was an ABC-TV interview with the Superintendent of Springs School, Peter M. Lisi. It followed Wednesday evening. The Associated Press also reported it had learned where Katie was from WLNG. ED.

At that point, Ricker realized he was wrong and apologized. He hoped he hadn't caused any problems for little Katie. "In retrospect," he said later, "I've always honored those embargoes. If they tell us to sit on a story, I have. But when I knew the TV stations were down there, I knew it would be on the local news. I was taking a chance. Had they not announced it that night, I would have felt bad. It took some of the sting out by saying it first. My feeling was she should have her privacy, but when I knew the TV cameras were there, they wouldn't honor it. I took a chance, that's what it amounts to."

Katie was upset by the attention. "Why do they want to take my picture?" she asked her foster family and her court-appointed lawyer, Anthony DiSanti. None of them had a ready answer except to note that the press has since, for the most part, turned to other stories. Katie continues to go to school freely. Other students don't treat her differently and her life continues.

There was some good to come out of the East Hampton Katie Beers flap. Sergeant Kenneth Brown, who handled the media onslaught, got what cops call a "good-guy" or "attaboy" letter:

> I wish to thank and congratulate you for the fine job in handling the Katie Beers matter. During a conversation with Peter Lisi, Superintendent Springs School, he had many generous comments concern-

ing the police department's efforts in containing the press. You deserve much of the credit for our performance.

I also note that many of the hours you put in were on your own time. You donated these hours to assist this unfortunate young lady.

Again, I thank you for this.

cc: Town Board
Personnel File
Capt. Sarris

Chapter Twenty-one

THE FAMILY COURT hearings continued periodically. A week after Marilyn Beers signed over temporary custody of her daughter, she won the right to regular visits. For the first three weeks, Marilyn and Helen were permitted to see Katie twice a week in the East Hampton foster home for one hour at a time. The third week, they were permitted three visits. At the end of the three weeks, Marilyn would meet with county officials in family court for another round of hearings.

But trouble was brewing between Marilyn and her attorney. Outside the courtroom, John Jiras made no secret of his interest in securing a movie deal for his client.

"Are you going to sell Katie's story?" a reporter asked.

"Is the Pope Catholic?" Jiras quipped.

Jiras's unremitting pressure to negotiate a film deal proved his undoing. Shortly after the hearing, Marilyn dropped him and retained Andrea Lannak, a Sayville attorney. Marilyn and Teddy had been discussing it for several days. They believed Lannak had the expertise they needed. "I'd rather be poor and have my daughter back than be rich and not have her," she told him.

At the same time, Marilyn announced that she was waiving control of Katie's finances—including movie deals—asking that all decisions be made by the Suffolk County attorney, Robert Cimino. He, in turn, named the county public administrator, Anthony Mastronardi, as temporary guardian of Katie's property.

At the next family court hearing Marilyn and Lannak slipped past reporters and photographers by entering through the nearby district court. Marilyn was sporting a new look: she'd cut ten inches off her straight brown hair and gotten a perm. *Newsday* ran a story about the Beers makeover.

Inside the courthouse, Lannak disappeared into Judge James F. X. Doyle's third-floor chambers for a closed-session meeting with county CPS authorities and Katie's legal guardian. Meanwhile, Marilyn chain-smoked in the ladies' room, carefully avoiding eye contact with the two reporters inside.

Finally, one of them spoke. "I won't bother you," the TV reporter said.

"Thank you," Marilyn said, with a slight smile.

"I won't bother you either," a magazine reporter added.

Marilyn laughed. "You two are probably the only ones."

The three women eyed each other for a moment. Marilyn broke the silence. "Can I have your cards?" she asked. "My son is collecting them."

As journalists waited in the courtroom they traded gossip. It was a busy day for the press: word had spread earlier that morning that Amy Fisher's alleged lover, Joey Buttafuoco, might be indicted on statutory rape charges, and a Lufthansa airliner had been hijacked and was headed for Kennedy Airport.

Anthony DiSanti, Katie's court-appointed lawyer, chatted briefly with the press. He said that he had spoken to Katie several times and she had told him whom she wanted to live with. DiSanti shook his head when reporters pressed for Katie's choice. "I can't say," he said. "But I can say that she loves her mother very much."

After several hours, a veteran *Newsday* photographer entered the room, tired of waiting to snap Marilyn leaving court. It was too cold outside, he said. He motioned to the judge's chambers.

"What the hell are they doing in there?" he asked.

"They're going to cut the kid in half," one reporter quipped. "Judge Solomon's in there."

The photographer sighed. It was turning out to be a long morning. "Guess I'll go back out," he said. "We're out there watching everyone get tickets—everyone who parked in handicapped."

The reporters exchanged uneasy glances. The photographer smirked and disappeared into the hallway.

It was almost 12:30 before the judge and the attorneys returned to the courtroom. The open-session part of the hearing lasted just five minutes.

"You are Marilyn Beers?" the judge asked.

"Yes, sir."

"I understand there has been an agreement between the three parties, Marilyn Beers, the County and the legal guardian," he said. "You have your rights, the county has its rights, and the legal guardian has the rights of the child. I want you to understand that I'm going to use my authority to ensure Katie is safe from any jeopardy. I want Katie to understand this court is here for her. I want her to know I have [ways of telling if] her needs have been properly met."

The judge increased Marilyn's visitation and agreed to meet again to discuss Katie's situation. Outside the courthouse, Marilyn swept past reporters, but Lannak stayed behind to answer questions. She said that Marilyn wanted to work with Katie's guardians to bring her home as quickly as possible. "Katie's already had enough pain," Lannak said. "Marilyn Beers wants Katie protected. It is certainly our understanding she wants to be with her mother."

Lannak brushed off reporters' questions of whether Linda Inghilleri might fight for custody of Katie. "I don't know why you give Mrs. Inghilleri so much notice," she said. "She is not in any position to gain custody. She is not a relative. I don't think it merits discussion."

Meanwhile, Sal Inghilleri continued to make news. Siben & Siben dropped him as a client, giving him back the retainer he had paid the previous year. Throughout the weeks Katie was missing, the attorneys had all suspected he was behind her disappearance.

"We thought Inghilleri did it," said Sidney Siben. "He had a motive—she was charging him with sexual abuse."

Even when they learned it was their other client—Esposito—the Sibens had had enough. "We told Inghilleri to take his money and go," Sidney Siben said. "It was embarrassing."

Sal said he didn't care. He got a new lawyer, and is now awaiting trial. He is confident he will be vindicated. "I ain't worried at all," he told reporters.

A week after his arrest, John Esposito, looking pale and unshaven in a gray suit and a white shirt, closed his eyes and hung his head as Judge Joel Lefkowitz upped his bail to $1.1 million. Prosecutors hit John Esposito with a total of eleven charges: three counts of first-degree kidnapping, six counts of first-degree sex abuse, one count each of endangering the welfare of a child and making a false sworn statement. His bail increased $100,000 for each of the counts.

He was asked to provide samples of his handwriting, blood, and other body fluid. In exchange, Esposito's attorneys asked for access to any statements Esposito had made to the police.

Andrew Siben told reporters his client was distraught. "He looks very tired," he said. "He's under tremendous pressure, tremendous stress. I told him Katie is doing well. He was certainly happy to hear that. . . . This case does have a happy ending," he added, "with the child being safely found."

As he awaits trial, John Esposito sees a psychiatrist regularly, and occasionally reads the Bible. He is growing a beard and sleeps on a cot covered with tissue paper. Corrections officials will not give him sheets for fear he will kill himself.

His family visits regularly, often bringing him books, especially his favorites—mysteries. He tells them repeatedly how sorry he is for all the pain he has caused. Once, he cried as he told his sister-in-law Joyce what a mess he had made of everything. "I'm sorry I won't be able to buy you Christmas presents anymore," he said.

Life has quieted down for Lieutenant Dominick Varrone. The kidnapping task force has disbanded. The basement of the Fourth Precinct is no longer its headquarters. In fact, no remnants remain of what used to be the county's most important case. The blackboard detectives used to plot strategy now has a new message: It reads: TASK FORCE MISSION: FIND ELVIS.

Things look pretty much the same in Mastic. Outside, Katie's pink bicycle leans against the door, and old boxes, a broken hat rack, and beer cans litter the stairway. A Christmas wreath still hangs on the door, and the tree still stands in the living room, even though it is almost spring. Marilyn says she won't take down the decorations until Katie comes home.

Two months after Katie disappeared, Little John finally saw his sister. It was a snowy Saturday in February. Katie showed him around her new foster home. They hugged for a long time.

It is uncertain when Katie Beers will return to her mother, but many believe it will happen. It is clear, however, that there are many Suffolk County officials who don't want that to happen. "I think it's rather interesting she is staying with a law enforcement family," notes *Post* reporter Kieran Crowley. "I don't think it's a coincidence. I think they are keeping her as far away from all the people she had anything to do with before, and as much under the control of law enforcement, as possible. It's an interesting situation. What would you do if your teenage son said, 'He's molesting me. He gives me all this stuff. It's been going on for years'? It's like Nixon. Is Nixon a crook or is he just naive? Well, these families are trying to tell you that they are naive. There's not much money, and all of a sudden they are getting lavish gifts, and their kids are being taken on trips. And they are looking the other way."

What will happen to Katie? By all accounts she is thriving in her foster home, eating voraciously, doing well in school, playing happily with new friends. But Dr. Vincent J. Fontana, the medical director and pediatrician-in-chief at the New York Foundling Hospital, says it will be a difficult road to recovery. Fontana is the author of *Save the Family, Save the Child: What We Can Do to Help Children at Risk*.

Katie's early years were fraught with difficulties. Until recently, there was a complete role reversal—the child parented the adults. "The children are expected to satisfy the needs of the parent," Fontana says. "They become like adults in a child's body. They go on feeling this is normal."

One of the key problems, Fontana says, is that adults have a distorted perception of what child abuse really is.

"If a child is being abused—emotionally, sexually, educationally—these are difficult to go into court and prove beyond a reasonable doubt," he says. "The black-and-blue marks are on the inside. But they hurt just as much."

Children, he says, have few protectors. "They have no rights, no vote, no lobby," he says. "It's an uphill battle to try to convince citizens that the welfare and well-being of every child is everyone's responsibility. People say, 'Child abuse isn't my problem.' Well, it's everybody's problem. Abused children will wind up the perpetrators of violent crime later in life."

Fontana says he is encouraged that Katie's mother says she wants her daughter's life to be different from what it was, but he remains skeptical. "Being motivated . . . to actually make change is not that easy," he warns. "Attitude, lack of parenting skills, the inability to love, to recognize what your child needs—those changes don't come easy. You can't get it overnight. The mother needs psychological help. So does the child. You're dealing with a multi-troubled family—people who don't recognize the horror of the child's environment, people who don't recognize the needs of the child."

The doctor's prognosis is grim. "Once the child returns I'm afraid that environment may slowly rear its ugly head again and go back to the way it was before."

Yet those who have come to know Katie Beers believe there is hope: it emerges from the child herself. For Katie has proved to the world her inner strength. She is a special child, a little girl who not only fought for her survival in the darkness of John Esposito's dungeon, but who continues to fight to this day.

The bell rings. School is out. Some five hundred elementary students charge down the stairs of the two-story brick schoolhouse. They are all bundled in down jackets, their wool caps pulled down over their ears. This is no day to leave mittens dangling from coat sleeves on pieces of yarn. It is cold out; the Gulf Stream that usually brings warm air to the Hamptons is pounding the South Fork of eastern Long Island with a mean wind. The temperature is in the twenties and the children do not linger as they noisily clamber onto yellow buses or pile into warm cars driven by waiting parents.

One of the buses lets some students off a mile away. The boys run ahead, oblivious to the weather. Snow is on the ground. There are angels to be made, snowballs to be packed. The girls are not far behind. Soon they too forget the weather. They slide along on the ice patches, emulating the spangled skaters they saw on television the weekend before. When the boys throw snowballs at them, they do not retreat. They retaliate, deliberately walking up to the offender and washing his face with a handful of snow.

Finally the children get home, a five-minute

walk that takes half an hour if you are ten years old and having fun. It is an idyllic world, a wonderful place to be a child. And the joy on the face of one of the girls is proof of all that. This is all new to her, going to school, making friends, living in a community where parents make their children a hot breakfast before they pack them off to school. She has never before lived where there are rules, where she has to be in bed by a certain time, has to take baths, has to clean her room.

She has never before lived in what is normal America. Her life has been very different, some say out of Charles Dickens. And now for the first time she is finding out she can be loved. And cared for. And safe.

She is a famous child. She became known in the headlines as Katie Beers. Only don't call her Katie. Her name, she says, is Katherine.

AN IMPORTANT MESSAGE TO THE READERS OF THIS BOOK

The abduction and imprisonment of Katie Beers is a tragedy that has moved the nation—but it is far from being an isolated occurrence. Nor is it indicative of the overall problem of missing and exploited children, for indeed, there *is* no one incident or crime which can be used to generalize about this complex and insidious problem.

It is also important to be aware of the full range of services that *are* available to assist families in the event their child is abducted.

As a society, our efforts to prevent crimes against children have not kept pace with the increasing vulnerability of our young citizens. In May 1990 the U.S. Department of Justice released a study reporting that there were as many as:

- 114,600 attempted abductions of children by nonfamily members
- 4,600 abductions by nonfamily members reported to police
- 300 abductions by nonfamily members where the children were gone for long periods of time or were murdered
- 354,000 children abducted by family members
- 450,700 children who ran away
- 127,100 children who were thrown away
- 438,200 children who were lost, injured, or otherwise missing

The National Center for Missing and Exploited Children (NCMEC), established in 1984 as a private, nonprofit organization, serves as a clearinghouse of information on missing and exploited children; provides technical assistance to citizens and law enforcement agencies; offers training programs to law enforcement and social service professionals; distributes photographs and descriptions of missing children nationwide; coordinates child protection efforts with the private sector; networks with nonprofit service providers and state clearinghouses on missing persons; and provides information on effective state legislation to ensure the protection of children per 42 USC 5771 and 42 USC 5780.

A 24-hour, toll-free telephone line is open for those who have information on missing or exploited children: **1-800-THE-LOST** (1-800-843-5678). This number is available throughout the United States, Canada, and Mexico. The TDD line is 1-800-826-7653. The NCMEC business number is (703) 235-3900.

A number of publications addressing various aspects of the missing and exploited child issue are available free of charge in single copies by contacting the National Center for Missing and Exploited Children's Publications Department, 2101 Wilson Boulevard, Suite 550, Arlington, Virginia 22201-3052.

Families need to know that traditional messages of "Don't take candy from strangers," "Don't be a tattletale," and "Be respectful to adults, they know what they're doing" are incomplete and can lead to the abduction and sexual victimization of children. Children and families do not have to live in fear of these crimes, but they do need to be alert, cautious, and prepared. The key to child safety is communication. A child's best weapon against victimization is his or her ability to think and preparation to respond to potentially dangerous situations. By learning and following the safety tips listed below, children can empower themselves with the skills, knowledge, and abilities to better protect themselves.

BASIC RULES OF SAFETY FOR CHILDREN

As soon as your children can articulate a sentence, they can begin the process of learning how to protect themselves against abduction and exploitation.

Children should be taught:

- If you are in a public place, and you get separated from your parents, don't wander around looking for them. Go to a checkout counter, the security office, or the lost and found and quickly tell the person in charge that you have lost your mom and dad and need help in finding them.
- You should not get into a car or go anywhere with any person unless your parents have told you that it is okay.
- If someone follows you on foot or in a car, stay away from him or her. You don't need

to go near the car to talk to the people inside.

- Grownups and other older people who need help should not be asking children for help; they should be asking older people.
- No one should be asking you for directions or to look for a "lost puppy" or telling you that your mother or father is in trouble and that he will take you to them.
- If someone tries to take you somewhere, quickly get away from him (or her) and yell or scream. "This man is trying to take me away" or "This person is not my father (or mother)."
- You should try to use the "buddy system" and never go places alone.
- Always ask your parents' permission to leave the yard or play area or to go into someone's home.
- Never hitchhike or try to get a ride home with anyone unless your parents have told you it is okay to ride with him or her.
- No one should ask you to keep a special secret. If he or she does, tell your parents or teacher.
- If someone wants to take your picture, tell him or her NO and tell your parents or teacher.

- No one should touch you in the parts of the body covered by the bathing suit, nor should you touch anyone else in those areas. Your body is special and private.
- You can be assertive, and you have the right to say NO to someone who tries to take you somewhere, touches you, or makes you feel uncomfortable in any way.

WHAT YOU CAN DO TO PREVENT CHILD ABDUCTION AND EXPLOITATION

- Know where your children are at all times. Be familiar with their friends and daily activities.
- Be sensitive to changes in your children's behavior; they are a signal that you should sit down and talk to your children about what caused the changes.
- Be alert to a teenager or adult who is paying an unusual amount of attention to your children or giving them inappropriate or expensive gifts.
- Teach your children to trust their own

feelings, and assure them that they have the right to say NO to what they sense is wrong.

- Listen carefully to your children's fears, and be supportive in all your discussions with them.
- Teach your children that no one should approach them or touch them in a way that makes them feel uncomfortable. If someone does, they should tell the parents immediately.
- Be careful about babysitters and any other individuals who have custody of your children.
- Talk to your child in a calm and reasonable manner, being careful not to discuss the frightening details of what might happen to a child who does not follow the safety guidelines.
- Take an active interest in your children, and listen to them. And, most important, make your home a place of trust and support that fulfills your child's needs—so that he or she won't seek love and support from someone else.